TIMEOUT!

HEADS UP, BASEBALL FANS

HEAD-TO-HEAD BASEBALL is a very different kind of book; it has two fronts and no back. Choose the player you want to read about first, read his story, and then flip the book over and read about the other player.

In the stories, you'll read how two very different players from two very different backgrounds ended up in the major leagues. You'll get the inside scoop on the Seattle Mariners' main man, Ken Griffey, Junior, and the lowdown on the Chicago White Sox's sensational slugger, Frank Thomas. After reading both superstar stories, tackle the amazing center section of the book. This section has fantastic photos, complete statistics, and a comic strip, all of which show just how these two power hitters stack up against each other.

Okay, it's time for the first pitch. So pick Junior or Frank and get ready for all the Head-to-Head action!

Head-to-Head Baseball: Ken Griffey, Junior and Frank Thomas
A SPORTS ILLUSTRATED FOR KIDS publication/April 1996

SPORTS ILLUSTRATED FOR KIDS and KiDS are registered trademarks of Time Inc.

Cover and interior design by Miriam Dustin
Illustrations by Steve McGarry
Cover photographs by Tom DiPace

All rights reserved. Copyright © 1996 Time Inc.

No part of this book may be reproduced or transmitted in any form or by any means, electronic or mechanical, including photocopying, recording, or by any information storage and retrieval system, without permission in writing from the publisher.

For information, write: SPORTS ILLUSTRATED FOR KIDS

Head-to-Head Baseball: Ken Griffey, Junior and Frank Thomas is published by SPORTS ILLUSTRATED FOR KIDS, a division of Time Inc. Its trademark is registered in the U.S. Patent and Trademark Office and in other countries. SPORTS ILLUSTRATED FOR KIDS, 1271 Avenue of the Americas, New York, New York 10020

ISBN 1-886749-10-8

PRINTED IN THE UNITED STATES OF AMERICA
10 9 8 7 6 5 4 3 2 1

Head-to-Head Baseball: Ken Griffey, Junior and Frank Thomas is a production of **SPORTS ILLUSTRATED FOR KIDS Books**: Cathrine Wolf, Editorial Director; Margaret Sieck, Senior Editor (Project Editor); Jill Safro, Associate Editor; Sherie Holder, Assistant Editor

Time Inc. New Business Development: David Gitow, Director; Stuart Hotchkiss, Associate Director; Peter Shapiro, Assistant Director; Mary Warner McGrade, Fufillment Director; Bob Fox, John Sandklev, Development Managers; John Calvano, Operations Manager; Donna Miano-Ferrara, Production Manager; Mike Holahan, Allison Weiss, Associate Development Managers; Dawn Weland, Assistant Development Manager; Charlotte Siddiqui, Marketing Assistant

KEN GRIFFEY, JUNIOR

by John Rolfe

A Sports Illustrated For Kids Book

CONTENTS

1. Refuse to Lose..........................6
2. Born to Play Ball......................12
3. Pros and Cons 21
4. Griffey Doubleheader 30
5. A Roller-Coaster Ride..................38
6. The Streak............................46
7. The Strike 51
8. Saving Seattle 58

   Ken Griffey, Junior's Career Stats 64

REFUSE TO LOSE

Ken Griffey, Junior, stood at home plate as the roar of 57,411 fans filled the Kingdome, in Seattle, Washington, on the night of October 8, 1995. Junior, a centerfielder for the Seattle Mariners, was facing the most important at-bat of his career.

The Mariners were trailing the New York Yankees, 5–4, in the bottom of the 11th inning of the fifth and final game of the American League division championship series. There were no outs and a runner was on first base. More than just a game was at stake. The Mariners were chasing a dream.

After having only two winning seasons in its 19-year history, the team had come close to moving to another city because attendance at its home games was so poor. Then, in 1995, the Mariners were amazing. They were 12½ games behind the first-place California Angels on August 15, but they did not give up. That day, Junior returned to the team after missing most of the season because of a broken wrist. The Mariners then went on to win 27 of their last 43 games

KEN GRIFFEY, JR.   7

in the season and catch the Angels, who had gone into a terrible slump. The two teams finished the season in a tie.

After beating California in a one-game playoff on October 2, Seattle advanced to the best-of-five division series against the American League East champion Yankees. The Mariners lost the first two games, but battled back to win two and force a fifth and deciding game. By that time, the people of Seattle were madly in love with the Mariners. They adopted the slogan REFUSE TO LOSE. That's just what the Mariners did against the Yankees.

Junior was the man Mariner fans wanted at bat during that big moment in the 11th inning of the deciding game of the series against New York. He was the best player the team ever had. He had already set an American League playoff record by belting five home runs in the five games (including one earlier in this game) against the Yankees. If he could hit another, the Mariners would be on their way to play the Cleveland Indians in the league championship series.

Junior was ready as Yankee pitcher Jack McDowell wound up and fired. Base hit to centerfield! Runners were now on first and second. Junior had become the potential winning run.

Moments later, Edgar Martinez, the Seattle designated hitter, smacked a hit into leftfield, and Junior took off at top speed. He raced around second and headed for third as the runner ahead of him scored the tying run. Junior kept going. A throw was on its way toward the plate as Junior raced home. The crowd held its breath as Junior slid . . .

Safe! The Mariners had won, 6–5!

Junior was quickly mobbed by his joyous teammates as the Kingdome exploded with deafening cheers. It was a moment few baseball fans will ever forget.

The Mariners later lost the American League Championship Series to the Indians, but that defeat did not erase the magic of the thrilling game — and series — against the Yankees. The Mariners had become Seattle's heroes at long last. It was only fitting that Junior had been the one who scored the winning run.

Junior is more than just the best Mariner player ever. Many people think he is the best player in the major leagues. In 1994, *Sports Illustrated* asked 15 major league managers and executives a question: If you could have any player who is no older than 25 play for your team for the next 10 years, whom would you choose? All of them chose Junior.

"All around, I would say he's the best and his defense is incredible," says two-time American League MVP Frank Thomas of the Chicago White Sox. "He's a natural. This is the guy who was born into this game."

Frank is right. Junior's dad, Ken senior, played for 19 seasons between 1973 and 1991. He was named to the All-Star team three times and was the MVP of the 1980 Game. He batted .296 while rapping out 2,143 hits, 152

KEN GRIFFEY, JR.

homers, and 859 RBIs during his career. He retired after the 1991 season.

Junior, who is now 26, is well on his way to topping his dad's accomplishments. After only seven seasons in the majors, Junior has already:

- Batted .300 or higher in a season five times;
- Driven in 100 runs or more in a season three times and has 585 career RBIs;
- Hit 20 or more homers in a season five times (including 40 or more twice) for a career total of 189;
- Won six Gold Glove Awards for fielding excellence;
- Played in five All-Star Games and was named All-Star MVP in 1992;
- Tied a major league record by hitting home runs

HEAD TO HEAD

Ken and Frank are both "Juniors." They were named after their fathers. However, Frank's dad never played pro baseball. Ken junior and his dad are one of at least 10 fathers and sons who have played in the major leagues. Current stars whose dads were big leaguers include Barry Bonds, Roberto and Sandy Alomar, Moises Alou, Todd Hundley, Bret Boone, Brian McRae, and Todd Stottlemyre.

in eight games in a row in 1993.

In 1994, Junior had hit 40 homers by the middle of August and had a chance to break Roger Maris's single-season home run record of 61. Unfortunately, the major league players went on strike on August 12th and the season was canceled a month later.

"Junior can do pretty much whatever he wants to, whenever he wants to do it," says Mariner designated hitter Edgar Martinez. "His swing is perfect. I would love to have his swing." Edgar, by the way, won the American League batting title in 1992 and 1995!

Ken senior, of course, is quite impressed with Junior, too. "Like everyone else, I am amazed," he says. "I'm in awe of him. He's doing things I could never do."

Junior is often compared to such Hall of Fame players as Willie Mays, Joe DiMaggio, and Ted Williams. Willie was a speedy, slugging centerfielder who was nicknamed "The Say Hey Kid." Joe was called "The Yankee Clipper" because of his fielding grace with the New York Yankees. Ted Williams batted .406 in 1941 and is the last player to bat .400 or higher over a season. His nickname was "The Kid," which is one of Ken junior's nicknames, too.

Junior, the latest "Kid" on the big-league block, makes everything he does look easy. Most players spend about five years in the minor leagues before they reach the majors. Junior spent only two before he made the Mariner roster in spring training of 1989.

Junior isn't amazed by his success. He thinks people make baseball too complicated. "You hit the ball, you run, you go after it, and you catch it," he says. "It's a simple game, really. I was born with this talent. I can't help it if I make things look easy that some people think are difficult."

"All of us would like to be able to keep the game that simple," says Cal Ripken, Junior, a 13-time All-Star shortstop for the Baltimore Orioles. "But only players with unbelievable natural talent can just go out and do the things Junior does."

Fans love to watch all that natural talent at work. Junior is one of those rare athletes — like Michael Jordan — whom fans in every city root for.

In 1990, Junior became the first player in Mariner history to be chosen by fans to start in the All-Star Game. In 1994, he received more All-Star votes (6,079,688) from fans than any player ever.

A big reason that fans love Junior so much is that he always looks as if he's having fun. He wears his cap backward during warmups. His face is often lit up by a beaming smile. He loves clowning around with his teammates, listening to rap music, and playing video games.

Junior's attitude toward baseball is something that he learned from his father. It's also what makes the Griffeys such a special baseball family. But even within that family, Ken Griffey, Junior, is in a category all his own.

BORN TO PLAY BALL

George Kenneth Griffey, Junior was born on November 21, 1969, in Donora, Pennsylvania. He was the first of Ken and Alberta Griffey's three children. A younger brother, Craig, was born a year later and a younger sister, Lathesia, came along two years after Craig.

Donora is a town of about 7,500 people located near the city of Pittsburgh, in southwestern Pennsylvania. It is famous for being the birthplace of Hall of Fame outfielder Stan Musial, who played for the St. Louis Cardinals from 1941 to 1963. Ken senior was also born in Donora, and his dad, Buddy, played baseball with Stan the Man in high school. There he also met his future wife, Alberta, who is known as "Birdie."

Ken senior was just beginning his first season of professional baseball, with a Cincinnati Reds minor league team, when Junior was born. His salary was only $500 per month, so he had to do odd jobs during the off-season to make ends meet. When no work was available, the Griffeys received welfare payments from the government.

Ken senior tried hard to be a good father. His own dad had left home when Ken was only 2 years old. Growing up without his dad made Ken senior want to be the father to his kids that he never had.

"Hopefully, I did a good enough job that they know right from wrong," he says.

Junior showed signs of physical talent at a very early age. He started walking when he was only seven months old! Most babies don't start to walk until they are 12 months old.

Junior's dream of being a major leaguer like his dad began as soon as he learned how to play baseball at age 4 or 5. But Ken senior never forced his children to play sports.

"I don't believe in pressuring kids," Ken senior says. "I told the boys, 'If you want to play, if you need some help, let me know.' With Junior, you could see it was what he wanted and how much fun he was having playing it. Craig didn't like the game. There was no reason to force it on him."

Junior also played football, basketball, and soccer with Craig when they got older. Football was Craig's favorite sport. He later went on to play defensive back at Ohio State University. After college, he switched to baseball and is now an outfielder for one of the Mariners' minor league teams.

Ken senior made it to the Cincinnati Reds in 1973 and started to make a lot more money. He moved the family

14 KEN GRIFFEY, JR.

to Cincinnati, where they lived in a nice house in the suburb of Mount Airy. It had a big family room with a spot for Ken senior to display his trophies. In the basement, there was an exercise room with weight machines.

Ken senior quickly became an important player for the famous Reds teams that were known as "The Big Red Machine" because of their powerful hitters. During the 1970's, the Reds won six National League West division titles and the World Series in 1975 and 1976.

Ken senior batted over .300 in both of those championship years, and he made more money than ever before.

HEAD TO HEAD

In 1979, the year Junior turned 10 years old:
- The Pittsburgh Pirates defeated the Baltimore Orioles in the World Series, 4 games to 3.
- Iranian militants took over the U.S. Embassy in Teheran and held 53 Americans hostage for 444 days.
- Baggy pants and roller-skating were hot fads.
- The Sony Walkman tape cassette player was first introduced.
- Frank Thomas was an 11-year-old growing up in Columbus, Georgia, where he was involved in football, basketball, and baseball.

He bought a Rolls Royce. Junior sometimes showed up for his Little League games in the Rolls, driven by his mom! When Junior turned 16, in 1988, his dad bought him an expensive BMW car. "My dad would give you the shirt off his back," Junior says. "I was spoiled."

Ken senior agrees. "Junior was spoiled," he says. "But I didn't mind spoiling him. A lot of things he did, I didn't get a chance to do when I was that age."

Having a dad who was a big-league ballplayer gave Junior the chance to do many things most kids never get to do. He hung out at the ballpark with his dad, met famous players, and played on the field with their sons. He went to the World Series in 1975, when he was 6.

Junior says he was never awed by the players many people worshipped as heroes. "They were just people my dad worked with," Junior says. "I didn't walk around thinking, 'Wow, these are the Cincinnati Reds.' My dad told me, 'Don't copy them. Just be yourself.'"

Junior says he never thought of his dad as a major league star. If you talk to Birdie, though, she'll tell you Junior was impressed by his dad all the time. She says he knew what his dad's batting average was on any given day and that Junior got upset whenever the Reds lost.

When Junior and his dad played catch in the backyard, sometimes mom joined in the fun. Birdie was a good athlete. She had played basketball and volleyball when she was in high school and later won a home-run-hitting contest against the wives of other players.

"She used to play catch with me, but one day I threw hard and smoked her hand," Junior says. "She threw down the glove, and that was the last time she caught for me!"

Junior had a lot of natural talent for baseball but also benefited by being able to watch his dad play. "I watched my dad play for years," he says. "I talked to him every day about the game. There isn't one thing I've seen so far that he hasn't told me about before."

Junior started playing Little League baseball when he was 8. He and Craig were teammates that year on the Mount Airy D team of the Class D Knothole League. Craig played centerfield and back-up catcher. Junior pitched and often threw so hard that kids went to bat in tears because they were so afraid of being hit by a pitch.

Once Junior got started in Little League, Ken senior did not interfere with his son's coaches. He let them teach Junior whatever they thought he needed to learn. Ken senior's biggest efforts were at instilling confidence in Junior.

"I always talked to Kenny about his mental outlook," Ken senior says. "Questions like, 'How positive are you about yourself?' 'How much confidence do you have in yourself and what you want to do?' I always told him that no one was ever going to hit, run, and throw for him. You have to have confidence in those things."

Most of all, Ken senior made sure that his son did not

take baseball too seriously. "[Dad] always used to tell me to go out and have fun, no matter what," Junior says.

Junior became so good by the time he was 11 that his dad could not strike him out. But Junior got so used to success that failure took him by complete surprise.

In one Little League game, he hit a hard shot, but the ball was caught by the first baseman. "I cried so hard they had to take me out of the game," Junior says.

Birdie rushed over and tried to comfort her son, "Look, your father makes plenty of outs," she said. "One out is not going to make any difference."

Junior looked at his mom and cried, "But that's him, that's not me!"

The Griffeys' lives changed in 1981. Less than three weeks before Junior's 12th birthday, the Reds traded Ken senior to the New York Yankees. The Griffey family stayed in Cincinnati, so Junior didn't get to see his dad very much during the baseball season.

While his dad was away, Junior kept in touch by talking with him on the phone. It became a habit, one that Junior became known for after he began his own pro career.

During the season, Junior and his family occasionally visited Dad in New York City. Junior made some friends on the Yankees. One of them was outfielder Rickey Henderson. Rickey became Junior's favorite player, and they even played one-on-one basketball together.

"Rickey gave me my first talk about baseball other than my father," Junior says. "He told me, 'You're going to be here in the majors someday. Stay away from the wrong crowd. If somebody does drugs, his name may not be mentioned, but yours will.'"

As they had done regularly in Cincinnati, Junior and his dad went to the ballpark to work out in the outfield and take batting practice. During those visits to Yankee Stadium, Junior made an impression on his father's teammates. They could tell he was going to be special.

"As a fifteen-year-old, Junior walked around with that little bit of a swagger," says Scott Bradley, who played for the Yankees in 1985 and later became Junior's teammate on the Mariners. "He knew how good he was."

By age 16, Junior was good enough to compete against 18-year-olds in Connie Mack League baseball. (Connie Mack is a league for kids ages 18 and under.) In the 1986 Connie Mack World Series, Junior hit three homers in one game: one to leftfield, one to center, and one to right!

Birdie kept telling Ken senior how good Junior was, but he had a hard time believing it because he was able to go to only a few of Junior's games between 1981 and 1988.

As a teenager, Ken junior had a complete case of sports on the brain. Unfortunately, he didn't pay much attention to his schoolwork. Junior's grades were so bad that when he entered Archbishop Moeller High School, he had to sit out his freshman year of baseball. Then he missed

KEN GRIFFEY, JR.

his sophomore season because he decided to go to spring training in Florida with his dad.

It wasn't until his junior season that Ken junior finally began to play high school baseball. That is very late for anyone who hopes to make it to the majors, but Junior made up for lost time during his first year of high school sports. He batted .478 with 11 homers. He grew six inches to 6' 3", and gained 40 pounds. His new size also helped make him a star wide receiver on the school football team.

Junior's dislike of being tackled made him decide to quit football his senior year, even though the team had won the Ohio state championship the year before. It also made more sense for him to concentrate on baseball because he had so much talent.

Mike Cameron, Junior's high school baseball coach, says Junior was the best player he ever coached during his 20 years at Moeller High. That's a big compliment. Several major league stars, such as Reds shortstop Barry Larkin, have played at Moeller.

Junior belted three home runs in one game and set a school record with 20 career homers during his two seasons at Moeller. He was also a dazzling fielder who could catch long fly balls while running full speed with his back to home plate. Major league scouts were wild about Junior, but the attention he received from them did not faze him at all. That is *not* to say he was never fazed.

"Only when his father was there would Kenny

pressure himself," Coach Cameron says. "A hundred scouts could be in the stands and it wouldn't make a difference. But not his father."

Junior could not seem to get a hit when his dad was watching. "When he was there, it was the only time I thought I had to impress somebody," Junior says.

Ken senior says, "I told him he never had to impress me. As long as he was happy, I didn't care. If he was a garbage man, that was fine with me."

In his senior year, Junior set a school record by batting .478 and had 7 homers and 28 RBIs in 24 games. He also stole 13 bases without being thrown out. Mariner scouts graded Junior's talent and gave him scores between 63 and 73. In their grading system, a score between 50 and 59 meant a player was a potential All-Star!

On June 2, 1987, when he was 17, the Mariners made Junior the first player chosen in the major league draft of amateur players. He was the first son of a major league player to be chosen first. Junior had also received a scholarship offer from Florida State University, but he wasn't about to turn down the major leagues, not after they chose him first!

With his dad acting as his agent, Junior agreed to a minor league contract that paid him a bonus of $160,000 just to sign the paper! Mariner officials then told Junior, "We want you in the majors in three years."

Making the majors that quickly is tough, but as it turned out, the Mariners didn't have to wait too long.

PROS AND CONS

The beginning of Junior's pro career planted the seed of a dream in his father's mind. Would it be possible that one day they might be able to play in the major leagues together?

It wasn't likely to happen. At the time, Ken senior was 37 years old. He had been traded to the Atlanta Braves in 1986 and the end of his career was in sight. Few players are still physically able to play in the majors after 35. Even so, he told his son, "You hurry up and I'll try to hang on. Maybe we can play together."

Ken senior knew that life in the minor leagues would be a big adjustment for Junior, who had never lived away from home before. Ken senior told reporters, "If he has any problems, he can give me a call. I'll call him every day, too, to make sure he's all right."

The Mariners sent Junior to their rookie minor league team, in Bellingham, Washington. (Rookie League is the lowest level of minor league baseball.) Bellingham is about 90 miles north of Seattle. Junior's team often took long bus rides (some up to 10 hours) to play in the neighboring states of Oregon and Idaho. The team bus was almost 30 years old. It had no bathroom and was very uncomfortable. On Junior's first long trip, he coped with the boredom and discomfort by climbing into the overhead luggage rack and going to sleep!

There were all kinds of surprises and trouble waiting for Junior that season. He had run-ins with the teenage sons of the team's bus driver. Junior told reporters that one of them called him "nigger" and another went looking for him with a gun. He was finding his new life in the minors to be pretty miserable.

"To be honest with you, it was a whole lot worse than I ever imagined," Junior says. "I didn't know what to do. All I knew is I wanted to go home."

Junior turned to his family for support. He started calling home so much his phone bill was $600 a month! His unhappiness affected his performance on the field. He fell into a slump and when his batting average dropped to .230, his mom flew to Bellingham.

Birdie was unhappy to learn that Junior had been benched for breaking a team rule against staying out too late at night and that he was thinking about quitting.

"I knew he needed some sympathy, but I got mad and told him to concentrate on his career," Birdie says. "The night before I left, I gave it to him up one side and down the

KEN GRIFFEY, JR. 23

other. He didn't call me for four days."

Rick Sweet, the team's manager, said Junior needed to grow up and keep his mind on the game. Junior often failed to hustle or lazily caught fly balls with one hand.

Junior agreed. "I have to mature," he said "That's why I'm here."

And mature he did: His first hit was a home run on June 17, 1987. He finished the season as the team's leader in batting average (.313), homers (14), and RBIs (43). *Baseball America* magazine rated him as the number-one prospect in the minor leagues.

Junior's first season of pro ball ended better than it had begun, but the rocky times continued. When he returned home, he began having arguments with his dad. Now that Junior was a professional, Ken senior expected his son to act more grown up and be responsible.

"Dad wanted me to pay rent or get my own place," Junior later told reporter Bob Finnigan of *The Seattle Times* newspaper in 1992. "I was confused. I was hurting and I wanted to cause some hurt for others."

Junior told the reporter that in January 1988, he tried to kill himself by swallowing 277 aspirin tablets. Junior's girlfriend and her brother tried to stop him from taking the pills, but were unsuccessful. Junior then got into his car, but threw up before he could drive away. His girlfriend's mother then drove him to the hospital.

Afterward, Junior and his dad worked out their differences by having long heart-to-heart talks. Junior later decided to talk to a reporter about the incident because he hoped that it might make other people realize that killing themselves is no way to solve problems in life. With time and help, things can always get better.

Junior no longer talks about his suicide attempt. In 1994, his dad told sportswriter Steve Marantz of *The Sporting News*, "We don't worry about it anymore. He was just like any other teen-aged kid. We moved on."

The Griffeys did move on — to much brighter times in 1988. Junior began the regular season with the San Bernardino Spirit of the Class A California League. He was such a hit in San Bernardino that the team held a KEN GRIFFEY, JR. POSTER NIGHT and it was a sellout.

One night in April 1988, Ken senior got his first good look at how well his son was playing. About 2,500 fans were at Fiscalini Field that night to see the Spirit take on a team from Palm Springs. Junior was leading the California League with a .520 batting average, four homers, and 11 RBIs. When he went to bat for the first time, the stadium announcer boomed, "Yes, indeedy, boys and girls, what time is it?"

"It's Griffey time!" roared the fans.

Ken senior shook his head. He couldn't believe what he was seeing and hearing!

As usual, Junior felt nervous with his dad there.

Between pitches, he sneaked a peek at Ken senior, who was sitting in the stands. With the count at two balls and one strike, Junior bunted the ball down the third-base line. He raced safely to first before the third baseman could make a throw. In the stands, his father grinned.

"I was going to get at least one hit," Junior later told reporters, "even if he gets on me about having to bunt."

In the sixth inning, team officials invited Ken senior to move up to the radio-broadcast booth. When the stadium announcer introduced Ken senior to the crowd, there were loud cheers. Junior was reminded of his dad's presence and

HEAD TO HEAD

Baseball players get training and experience in the minor leagues. Each major league team has between six and eight minor league teams that develop or "grow" players for it. That is why these minor league teams are called "farm teams."

Junior and Frank each spent less than two full seasons in the minors. Making the majors without playing in the minors at all is a rare accomplishment. Only 17 players—including California Angel pitcher Jim Abbott and Blue Jay first baseman John Olerud—have done so since the major league draft was started, in 1965.

struck out in his next at-bat.

In the eighth inning, the Spirit were ahead, 9–5, when Junior went to bat, with two out and no runners on base. He was so desperate to get a good, solid hit that he used his third bat of the game!

With the count at three balls and two strikes, Junior blasted a fastball deep to leftfield. The outfielder ran back, but the ball sailed over the fence and landed in a clump of trees more than 400 feet from home plate.

In the radio booth, Ken senior put his hand to his mouth and mumbled, "Did you see how far that ball went?"

When Junior crossed home plate, he pointed up at his dad as if to say, "See? How did you like that?"

After 58 games, Junior was batting .338, with 42 RBIs, and leading the league with 11 homers and 32 stolen bases. Then he tried to make a diving catch and strained his back. On June 9, he was placed on the disabled list, and he didn't play again until August 15. With the end of the season approaching, the Mariners decided to promote him to their Double A team in Vermont.

Junior did well at the next higher minor league level, even though his back was still so sore he could only play as a designated hitter. In 17 games, he hit .279, with two homers and 10 RBIs.

Junior's fine season showed that he had the talent to rise through the minors quickly. But could he rise quickly

KEN GRIFFEY, JR. 27

enough to make the majors while his dad was still there? Time was running out for Ken senior.

When spring training began in 1989, there was a good chance that not even one Griffey would play in the major leagues that season.

Ken senior had been released by the Braves in July of the year before. In August, he got another shot with the Reds, signing on as a free agent, but he didn't play much during the rest of the 1988 season. He knew he would have to have a very good spring if he wanted to stay on the team.

Before training camp, Ken senior said to his son, "Hurry up and make it [to the majors]. This might be my last season."

Ken senior didn't really expect the two of them to be in the majors together. "It meant pressure on both of us," he says. "I had to be good enough to stick around. He had to be a heck of a player at his young age to get here that quickly."

The Mariners were impressed with Junior's progress, but they thought he needed one more season in the minors. Hopes for a Griffey family reunion on the field of dreams grew dim.

Junior was only three months past his 19th birthday when he reported to the Mariners' training camp, in Arizona. Manager Jim Lefebvre had heard a lot about him and was eager to see what Junior could do. Junior made Jim's eyes pop out by setting a Mariners' spring-training record by getting at least one hit in 15 straight games.

Junior's hot streak presented the Mariners with a tough decision about where he belonged. On the one hand, the team had never had a winning record since it joined the league in 1977. It needed a star to lift the team and to draw fans. On the other hand, team officials didn't want to rush Junior to the majors. They were worried that his confidence might be hurt or destroyed if he struggled and had to go back to the minors. They were also afraid that Junior might not be able to handle the pressure of being compared to his dad.

"I've seen guys with tremendous talent, but to say he can play day-to-day major league baseball at age nineteen is a heck of a statement," Jim told reporters. "If we rush him, it could set him back a couple of years."

Jim told Junior to relax and not worry about making the team. Relaxing wasn't easy. Junior had become one of the biggest stories in baseball that spring. Reporters from national newspapers, magazines, and TV shows followed him constantly.

Junior wanted very much to make the team. "I'll be upset if I don't make it, but it's up to them and I won't cause problems," he said. "I feel I can play every day right now, even though I know I still have lots to learn. I am a little amazed I've come this far this fast."

He *was* coming far — and fast. In all, Junior hit .359 in 26 exhibition games. He set team spring-training records with 33 hits and 21 RBIs. He also played great defense.

On March 29, Manager Jim Lefebvre asked Junior to step into his office.

"This is the most difficult decision a manager has to make," Jim said seriously. He watched Junior's spirits sink. Then Jim dropped the bomb: "You've made the team," he said. "Congratulations! You're my starting centerfielder."

Junior later told reporters how it felt to hear that great news. "My heart started ticking again," he said. "Those are probably the best words I've ever heard. At least in the top three."

"What are the other two?" a reporter asked.

"[When my parents said] 'You can keep the BMW,' and my parents telling me 'I love you,'" Junior replied.

When Junior called his Dad to tell him the big news, Ken senior was speechless.

"I just kept saying 'Dad? Dad? Dad?'" Junior says, "He didn't say anything."

The next day, Junior got more good news. Ken senior had done his part to fulfill the family dream by batting .333 in his first 21 at-bats that spring and had made the Reds! He had a one-year contract to play for them. The Griffeys were about to become the first father and son to play in the major leagues at the same time!

GRIFFEY DOUBLEHEADER

On April 3, Ken senior and the Reds opened the 1989 season in Cincinnati against the Los Angeles Dodgers. Later that day, Junior and the Mariners played the A's in Oakland. Ken senior didn't get a hit, but Junior cracked a double in his first official major league at-bat. The hit was extra special because Ken senior's first career big-league hit had also been a double.

Later that night, Ken senior saw a replay of Junior's hit on TV. "I'll tell you the truth, I cried," he says.

Junior's rookie season had begun in a blaze of glory. On April 10, he celebrated his dad's 39th birthday by bashing a home run against the Chicago White Sox at the Kingdome. It was Junior's first at-bat of the season in front of the Mariners' home fans, and he hit the homer with his first swing of the game.

After the game ended, Junior called his dad to say the homer was a birthday present. "You're not getting away that cheap," Ken senior laughed. "Send me a present through the mail."

On April 26 at the Kingdome, Junior displayed all of his talent against the Blue Jays. In the first inning, he blasted a line drive off the rightfield wall to drive in two runs. In the third, he smashed a double into the rightfield corner. Then, in the seventh, Junior pounded a pitch over the rightfield wall to give Seattle a 7–6 win.

Junior's hitting was only part of the story on that fabulous night. In the fifth inning, he made a running, over-the-shoulder catch on the warning track.

"Tonight, Ken Griffey was the living definition of the word *impact*," Jim Lefebvre said after the game. "What he showed out there is what it's all about, folks."

Junior wasn't impressed with what he had done. "This was nice, fun," he told reporters. "But it was only one game and one game does not make a career."

Meanwhile, Ken senior wasn't playing much for the Reds. But one day in early May, he got his first chance to start in a game and belted his first hit of the season. It was a home run. The game was shown live on the message board of the Kingdome while the Mariners were doing their pregame workout. When Junior saw his dad's homer, he happily high-fived his teammates.

The other Mariners got a kick out of Junior. "He's like a little brother to most of the guys," second-baseman Harold Reynolds said.

Junior loved to joke around and play pranks in the clubhouse. He drank soda instead of beer, and usually listened to rap music on headphones before games.

Sometimes the three Mariner outfielders gathered in the outfield while a new pitcher was warming up. Instead of discussing where they should play the next hitter, Junior would talk to his teammates about his favorite songs and rock bands.

"He has so much fun out there that he completely forgets what's going on," Gene Clines, the Mariner batting coach, said.

Junior was playing so well and fans loved his sweet personality so much that Steve Kelley, a sports columnist for *The Seattle Times*, wrote that Junior deserved to have a candy named after him. In May, the Pacific Trading Cards company introduced the Ken Griffey, Junior, chocolate bar.

Another popular "Junior item" was a poster of Junior and Ken senior posing together in their major

HEAD TO HEAD

In 1989, Junior made the Mariners at age 19 by batting .359, with 2 homers and 26 RBIs in 26 spring-training games. He also became the first player ever to play in the majors while his father was still an active player. Meanwhile, Frank was drafted by the White Sox that June out of Auburn University, in Alabama.

KEN GRIFFEY, JR.

league uniforms. Fans bought more than 30,000 copies of the poster during the first two weeks it was on sale.

Junior became so popular he had to refuse a dozen requests each week for appearances and product endorsements. Handling so much attention wasn't easy. The team had to limit his interviews to formal press conferences in cities where the team played on road trips.

"We want Junior to stay focused on baseball," Jim Lefebvre explained.

Unfortunately, Junior did not get the chance to do that for long. On July 25, he slipped and fell in the shower and broke a bone in the little finger on his left hand. He was batting .287, with 13 homers and 45 RBIs at the time. Many people thought he was a lock to win the American League Rookie of the Year award.

"It's pretty disappointing," Junior told reporters, referring to his injury, "but there's nothing I can do."

Junior was placed on the disabled list and did not play again until August 20. When he returned, he tried too hard to pick up where he had left off and it made him play poorly. By trying to hit homers, he ended up hitting only three and batted .181 in September and October.

"I was worrying about hitting the ball 700 feet," Junior explained. "I just wanted 20 home runs."

Junior finished his rookie season in the majors with 16 homers, 61 RBIs, 16 stolen bases, and a .264 batting average. When the Baseball Writers Association voted for the American League Rookie of the Year, Junior finished third, behind pitchers Gregg Olson of the Baltimore Orioles and Tom Gordon of the Kansas City Royals.

In his first major league season, Junior had shown brilliant flashes of talent. During the winter of 1989–90, he kept developing and gained 15 pounds, so he was 6' 3" and 195. Bigger and stronger, he got off to a roaring start the next season.

Junior was named the American League Player of the Month for April. He had hit .388, with 5 homers and 17 RBIs. By the middle of May, he was leading the league in hitting with a .370 average. He also became the first Mariner ever selected by fans across the country to start in an All-Star Game.

While Junior was in Chicago for the All-Star Game at Wrigley Field, in July, he was asked by a reporter to name the accomplishment that made him most proud.

"It's being in the big leagues and still having my dad here," Junior replied. "That means the most to me."

Little did Junior know that seven weeks later, having his dad "here" would mean "with the Mariners."

Things had not been going well for Ken senior. He had barely played at all after July 4th and hit only .206, with 1 homer and 8 RBIs. On August 18th, the Reds asked him to go on the disabled list even though he wasn't injured. The Reds wanted Ken senior to move in order to make a spot on the roster for another player.

Ken senior decided to retire instead. He figured that he had had a good, long career. He also wanted to be the one who decided when it was time for him to quit. However, someone else had a better idea.

On August 29, 1990, Ken senior was signed by the Mariners. He and Junior were now the first father and son ever to be active players for the same major league team.

Ken senior called it the best day of his career.

Junior told reporters that he had been pestering the team for two months about trading for his dad. "I didn't ask for him," he said. "It was more of a demand. I just told dad to get over here. I wanted him around."

Ken senior needed a couple of days to get ready for his first game with Seattle. On August 30, the day before he would actually play, the media started arriving at the Kingdome in huge numbers.

The excitement was building for the Griffeys, too. The afternoon before the game, Junior did some errands with his agent, Brian Goldberg. "It's really going to be weird tonight, playing with my dad," Junior said to Brian.

Two hours later, Brian drove Ken senior to the Kingdome. "You know," Ken senior said. "It's going to be weird tonight, playing with my son."

Finally, the big moment arrived. As the Griffeys trotted out to their positions in the outfield, Junior gave his dad a quick wave that could have been a salute.

"I didn't know what to expect," Ken senior says. "It was the most nerve-racking night I've ever spent in my life. I've always had butterflies, but it took a lot more concentration than I could have imagined."

The situation made Ken senior so shaky before he went to bat, he had to steady himself by holding on to the bat rack in the dugout. "Then I go to the plate and I heard, 'Come on, Dad!'" he says. "That really shook me up. After the first pitch, I settled down."

Royals pitcher Storm Davis threw a fastball, and Ken senior swung and singled to centerfield! Junior followed with a single of his own and the Griffeys were off and running. Ken senior later made a great defensive play, and the happy night was capped off by a 5–2 win.

"Like any other father, I was nervous because I wanted him to do well," Ken senior told reporters after the game. "I know he was just as excited as me."

"I didn't know what to think," Junior said. "I wanted to cry. I just stood there and looked at him in leftfield."

A week later, against Boston, Ken senior hit his first homer as a Mariner. Junior was waiting at the plate to greet him. Playing with Junior seemed to make Ken senior young again. He was named the American League Player of the Week, batting .632, with 1 home run and 7 RBIs. It was the first time in his 18-year career he had been named Player of the Week.

One of the most special moments of the season took

place on September 14 at Anaheim Stadium. In the first inning, Ken senior blasted a shot to centerfield off Angel pitcher Kirk McCaskill. Home run! When Ken senior crossed home plate, he high-fived Junior and said, "That's the way you do it, son."

Junior followed his dad's example by bashing a home run of his own.

Junior and his dad had a blast being teammates. Junior called his dad "Pops" and loved to walk past his locker and make a wise crack or ask for money. When he did, Ken senior threatened to spank him or tell mom.

In all, the Griffeys played together in 15 games that season, winning 7 and losing 8. Junior hit .312, with 3 homers and 11 RBIs in those games. Ken senior topped him by batting .400, with 3 homers and 16 RBIs.

"That was the best month I've had in the majors," Junior says. "We were having such a great time playing together, being teammates, playing baseball."

Ken senior said, "This is something to cherish."

Junior had some feats of his own to cherish. He had made his first All-Star team and won his first Gold Glove award. His final stats (.300 batting average, 22 homers, 80 RBIs) showed the promise of great things to come.

"He can be as good as he wants to be," said Ken senior.

How good did Junior want to be? That was a question he was forced to ask himself during his next season.

A ROLLER-COASTER RIDE

The 1991 season began with signs of trouble for the Griffeys. On March 2, Ken senior hurt his neck in a car accident in Phoenix, Arizona. It would keep him from playing regularly. Then the Mariners got off to a terrible start by losing their first six games of the season. They won their next eight, then lost five more in a row.

Losing games began to affect Junior. He hit only two homers and had just seven RBIs during the month of April. "I was down on myself," he says. "I wanted to win so bad, and when we didn't, it was like, 'Oh, no, not again.'" The Mariners were still the only team in the major leagues that had never had a winning season. A lot was expected of them that season. They had young, talented players such as outfielder Jay Buhner and starting pitcher Randy Johnson. Junior was supposed to lead the way, but he, and the team, struggled.

The season became a roller-coaster ride. The Mariners won 13 of their first 17 games in May. Junior perked up, too, and hit .300, with 4 homers and 15 RBIs during the month. But by June 1, there was more bad news. Ken senior's neck was hurting so much he had to go on the disabled list.

Junior struggled without his dad around. He hit only .226 during all of June. Second baseman Harold Reynolds noticed how tense Junior was becoming. One day, when the Mariners were on the road, Harold sat down next to Junior in the dugout during batting practice.

"Why are you putting so much pressure on yourself?" Harold asked him. "Just relax and have fun, and it'll happen."

It was hard for Junior to relax or have fun. By the All-Star break, in July, the Mariners were in sixth place in their division with a 40–42 record.

Junior was also hearing a lot of criticism. Sportswriters, and even some major leaguers, were accusing him of not playing as hard as he could.

Junior had heard that criticism before. Early in the 1990 season, Tiger manager Sparky Anderson had scolded him for not running hard to first base after hitting a ground ball. "You're lucky your dad didn't see you when you weren't hustling," Sparky had told him. "People pay money to see you play."

When Junior went to Toronto to play in the 1991 All-Star game, sportswriter Steve Kelley wrote an open letter to him in *The Seattle Times* newspaper. It pointed out that Junior had hit only .280, with 9 homers, 36 RBIs, and 46 strikeouts during the first half of the season. Those stats were not very good for a player many people thought of as the next Willie Mays.

"We have great expectations for you," Steve wrote. "But now we're beginning to wonder. We don't see the work habits of Willie Mays. We don't see the hunger that drove Mays into the Hall of Fame."

The letter also noted that Junior had been goofing off in batting practice, letting his mind wander during games, making mistakes like not throwing to the cutoff man, and barely running out grounders and fly balls.

"We wonder what a player would be like with your talent and your father's hunger," the columnist wrote. "Ken Griffey, Sr., runs harder to first base than you do. Willie Mays was a marvelously talented athlete, but he also worked incredibly hard. It seems as if you are just getting by with just your talent."

HEAD TO HEAD

In 1991, Junior batted .327, with 22 homers, and drove in 100 runs for the first time. Frank was playing his first full season with the White Sox and batted .318, with 32 homers and 109 RBIs. Junior made the American League All-Star team. Frank did not.

Steve added that Junior's contract guaranteed him a huge raise in salary — more than a million dollars — no matter how well he played. "Will you settle for being a multimillionaire instead of a Hall of Famer?" Steve asked. "Maybe now it's time to go to work. Time to be more than just a good player. Time to be great. But some of us wonder if you want it enough."

When Junior read Steve Kelley's letter, an alarm clock went off in his head. "The article made me think about what I was doing," he says.

Junior called Steve to talk about the article and later told reporters, "My intensity is always there, but maybe it doesn't always show. I want to be the best I can be."

Junior backed up his words by playing better than ever during the second half of the season. On July 23 at Yankee Stadium, he blasted his first career grand slam to power the Mariners to a 6–1 win. A week later, against the Orioles, he made a great running catch of a 405-foot drive, hit by Randy Milligan with the bases loaded. Then he went to bat in the bottom half of the inning and smacked another grand slam. The Mariners won, 8–2.

In July, Junior led the league in batting with a .434 average, hit five homers, and drove in 25 runs. Meanwhile, the Mariners boosted their record to 54–48.

"Since that article was written, he's done a lot of great things," manager Jim Lefebvre said. "It set him on fire."

42 KEN GRIFFEY, JR.

By August 16, the Mariners had 10 more wins than losses for the first time in their history. They were in fourth place, only five-and-a-half games behind the first-place Twins. Junior was honored as the American League Player of the Week for batting .542, with 3 homers and 9 RBIs.

"We knew he could do it all," Jim Lefebvre said. "Now he's doing it when it's never counted more."

For the first time in his big-league career, Junior was enjoying the excitement of winning and being in a pennant race. "It's a lot of fun," he told reporters. "This team is great. Everybody knows we're good and that if we play good, fundamental baseball, we can match up with every team."

Junior also downplayed his own accomplishments. "I'm not looking at my numbers," he said. "If you hit .200 and you win, or .300 and you win, it's all the same. Just so you win."

Unfortunately for the Mariners, the winning didn't continue. On August 20, they went to Minnesota for a big three-game showdown with the Twins. Seattle was six-and-a-half games behind and lost all three games. Then the Mariners were swept by the Tigers in their next three games in Detroit. Suddenly they were 10½ games out of first and their season was all but over.

Sadly, Ken senior's season was over too. He had gone to bat only 85 times all season. On August 31, he announced that he was going to have surgery on his neck. "I can't go any further without pain," he said. "It interferes with my hitting."

Ken senior was expected to be in the hospital for three days, and doctors had told him he could not be physically active for about three months. It was likely that his career was over.

Even though the season ended on a sour note, Junior and his teammates had some things to be proud of. The Mariners finished with an 83–79 record — their first winning record ever. Junior's second half of the season (.372, 13 homers, 64 RBIs) had been the best of any player in the league. His final stats included 22 homers, 100 RBIs, and team records for batting average (.327) and doubles (42). He also won his second Gold Glove.

Then Junior had to adjust to some important changes. In November, his dad announced his retirement after 19 seasons in the major leagues. The most surprising change came when the Mariners fired manager Jim Lefebvre. It was a strange move. Jim had just done something no one had ever done before: lead the Mariners to a winning season. He was replaced by Bill Plummer, starting with the 1992 season.

And what a disaster that season was! In 1992, the Mariners suffered a series of injuries to their best players and sank like a leaky boat. Even Junior got hurt. He sprained his right wrist while diving for a fly ball and went on the disabled list from June 9 to June 25. Seattle had a winning record on only one day that season (it was 10–9 on April 24). In September, it set a team record by losing 14 games in a row and ended up last in its division with a final record of 64–98. Bill Plummer was fired at the end of the season and Lou Piniella was chosen to be the team's new manager.

Lost in the shipwreck of the Mariners' season was another fine performance by Junior. He batted .308, reached new career-highs in homers (27) and RBIs (103), and won another Gold Glove.

The highlight of Junior's season came at the All-Star Game, in San Diego, at which he put another page in his family's history book.

There were four sons of big-leaguers in the American League lineup that night. The starting shortstop was Cal Ripken, Junior, of the Baltimore Orioles, whose dad had managed the Orioles from 1987 to April 1988. The starting catcher was Sandy Alomar, Junior, whose father had played various infield positions for different teams from 1964 to 1978. Sandy junior's brother Roberto started at second base. Junior played centerfield, of course, and shone brighter than all the other sons.

In the first inning, Junior singled in a run as the American League erupted for four runs. In the third inning, he belted a screaming drive over the leftfield fence. The home run made the Griffeys the first father and son to hit All-Star Game home runs. (Ken senior's had occurred 12 years earlier.)

In the sixth inning, Junior cracked a double to start another four-run rally. When he was taken out of the game at the end of the inning, the American League was on its way to a 13–6 victory.

Junior's big night became even sweeter when he was chosen the game's Most Valuable Player. He and his dad were now the first father and son to win the award.

"The award means a lot," Junior said afterward. "I just wanted to come out and play and do the best job I could for the American League. I certainly wasn't thinking about MVP."

"He's a very talented kid," said Tom Kelly of the Twins, who managed the American League team. "He's going to be a big-numbers kind of guy."

Tom Kelly was right. In 1993, Junior became a big-numbers guy — especially in the home run department.

6

THE STREAK

After three full seasons in the majors, Junior had established himself as a mighty power hitter. In 1992, Mariner outfielder Kevin Mitchell told reporters, "I've seen the man on the bench, in a tie game, say to me, 'Do you want me to hit a home run?' Then he does it."

In 1993, Junior did it more than ever.

His first home run of the season came in his first at-bat on opening day in the Kingdome. After the first two months of the season, Junior had 10 homers and 30 RBIs. Pitchers became afraid to throw to him. He ended up setting a team record by being walked intentionally 25 times that season.

On June 20th, he began a streak of four straight games in which he hit a home run. By the All-Star break, in July, he had hit 22, and was again elected to the All-Star team.

The day before the All-Star Game at Camden Yards, in Baltimore, Junior treated the fans to an awesome display of power. He competed in a home-run-hitting contest with several other All-Stars, including outfielder Juan Gonzalez of the Texas Rangers. Each player tried to hit as many home runs as he could before failing to clear the fence 10 times.

Juan got the crowd buzzing by bombing a 473-foot drive off the upper deck in leftfield. He followed it by blasting a 455-foot shot off the wall behind the centerfield fence. No player had ever hit a ball there before, but Junior was not going to be outdone.

During his turn at bat, Junior launched a drive way over the rightfield fence. The ball carried until it hit the wall of a warehouse. The blast was estimated at 445 feet and it made Junior the first player ever to hit a ball off the building.

"I didn't think it was going to get there," he later told reporters. "I was trying to concentrate on the next pitch, then everybody started clapping."

Baseball fans really started clapping on July 20 when Junior began a run at one of baseball's most amazing records. He started that day by hitting a home run in the eighth inning at Yankee Stadium. The next day, he hit another homer off Yankee pitcher Jimmy Key, in the sixth inning.

The Mariners then traveled to Cleveland, where Junior smacked a homer in his next game. That gave him three home runs in three straight games. Something special was happening.

Junior kept pounding away. On July 27th, in Seattle, Junior blasted a 441-foot grand slam against the Twins to make it seven homers in seven straight games. He was now one homer away from tying the major league record set by Dale Long of the Pirates, in 1956, and Don Mattingly of the Yankees, in 1987.

Don was watching Junior's streak with a lot of interest. He had been a teammate of Ken senior's on the Yankees from 1982 to 1986. "It's kind of funny that this kid I watched shag fly balls and saw grow up has the chance to tie it or possibly break the record," Don told reporters. "It doesn't bother me at all. It's kind of cool."

On July 28th at the Kingdome, Junior took his shot at tying the record. He struck out in the first inning and grounded out to first base in the fourth. His third at-bat was the charm when he mashed the first pitch from Willie Banks of the Twins. The ball sailed high, far, and deep to rightfield. Junior grinned and watched as the ball bounced off the front of the third deck. Home run!

Junior happily bounded around the bases and was given a three-minute standing ovation by the crowd. He came out of the dugout twice to wave to the cheering fans, who gave him another ovation when he trotted out to his position at the end of the inning.

Now the big question became: Could Junior break the record?

Mariners first baseman Tino Martinez thought so. Tino told reporters, "He's playing way above everybody else in baseball right now."

KEN GRIFFEY, JR. 49

On July 29th, the eyes of the baseball world were on Seattle when the Mariners took on the Twins. A crowd of 45,607 fans showed up at the Kingdome and cheered Junior's every move.

In his first three at-bats, he hit a scorching single and a hard double, but time began to run out. In the seventh inning, Twins relief pitcher Larry Casian threw Junior a perfect pitch to hit for a home run. To everyone's surprise, Junior popped it up. He was out and never got to bat again. The streak was over.

Junior's streak was truly amazing. It's hard enough for players to get a hit in eight games in a row, let alone eight home runs. The streak also gave Junior 30 home runs for the season. The total was another career-high, and he still had two months left in the season.

Junior's spectacular hitting overshadowed another of

HEAD TO HEAD

Junior and Frank had monster seasons in 1993. Junior tied a major league record by blasting home runs in eight consecutive games and finished the season with 45. Frank smashed 41 homers, led the White Sox to the playoffs, and was named American League MVP. (Junior has never won that award.)

his great accomplishments that season. When he made an error on August 8th against Texas, few people realized it was the first one he had made since April 16, 1992. That was 240 games before! He had set a major league record for outfielders by handling 573 "chances" (fielding grounders and flies or making a throw) without an error.

On September 1, Junior hit his 40th homer of the season against the Tigers. He was now the first Mariner ever to reach that total in one season.

How was he doing it? Where were all these home runs coming from?

"I don't consider myself a homerun hitter," Junior told a reporter from *Sports Illustrated*. "But when I'm hitting the ball hard, it will go out of the park. During the streak, I didn't do anything differently than anyone else was doing. I just went up there and hit. And hit."

Junior finished the season with a team-record 45 home runs. He also batted .309, with 109 RBIs, and won his fourth Gold Glove. The 109 RBIs made him only the fourth player in big-league history to have 100 or more RBIs in a season three-straight times before reaching the age of 24.

There was no question that 1993 had been Junior's best season yet. It didn't seem possible that he could do much better than he had done that season, but he was just getting warmed up. The 1994 season was going to be a *real* blast!

THE STRIKE

The year 1994 began with great joy for Junior when his wife, Melissa, whom he had married in 1992, gave birth to a son on January 19.

Junior and Melissa talked about what to name their baby. The obvious choice was George Kenneth Griffey III. But that seemed too formal, so they chose Trey Kenneth instead. The word "trey" *[tray]* means "three."

Junior instantly fell in love with his baby. Ken senior, who was now a proud grandfather, noticed that being a father made Junior more responsible at home and even happier at the ballpark.

"He's changed a lot since he's become an old man," Ken senior said. "He doesn't want to be called Kid anymore."

When spring training began, Junior showed renewed hustle and determination. He started to study the game more closely and watched videotapes of his at-bats to see when he was swinging properly and when he was making mistakes.

It was clear that Junior was preparing himself for a monster season. A lot was expected of the Mariners, too.

Major League Baseball had split each league into three divisions instead of two. Seattle was in the new American League West with Oakland, California, and Texas. The Mariners had more than enough talent to finish ahead of those teams.

After the regular season opened, on April 4th, home runs started flying out of ballparks in record numbers. Junior hit eight homers in April and then roared through May, during which he had a streak of 8 in 10 games. By May 30th, he had hit 22 and broken the major league record for most homers during the first two months of a season. The record had been set by Hall of Famer Mickey Mantle, in 1956.

Junior was now on a pace to hit 74 homers in the season, which would break the single-season record of 61 set by Roger Maris of the Yankees in 1961.

Despite Junior's performance, the Mariners were having a hard time winning. They lost the first five games of the season, but because their division was weak, they wound up in first place at the end of April with an 11–13 record. Then came a disastrous slump.

The Mariners went to Oakland on May 23 and lost two out of three games to a team with a 4–27 record. The next stop was Milwaukee, where Seattle was swept in three games by the Brewers, who had just lost 14 in a row!

Junior became so frustrated he told a reporter from the *News Tribune* of Tacoma, "It takes heart to win and we don't have enough here to win the division. It's easier to roll over and quit. People say we've never won here and never will. For some players, it's easier to let it keep happening than try to change it."

Junior even threatened to leave the Mariners when his contract ended after the 1996 season. "I love Seattle," he said. "but losing is killing me."

Junior's anger lit a fire under his teammates. They went out the next day and thrashed the Twins, 12–0.

"I told Junior that I was happy to hear what he said," Lou Piniella said after the game. "It was the same theme I've tried to get across for a while, but sometimes players listen better to another player. Every player should be tired of losing. You play every day, and it's a grind. The more you win, the more fun you have. All the young man was saying is that he's tired of losing."

During the next month, Junior took out his anger on the baseball itself. On June 24th in the Kingdome, he blasted a 400-foot shot off pitcher Paul Assenmacher of the White Sox. It was Junior's 32nd homer as well as his 23rd 400-foot blast of the season.

"He said he was going to go deep," White Sox first baseman Frank Thomas told reporters after the game. "I could see it in his eyes, and he's definitely in a groove."

Frank was in a groove, too. During that weekend series in Seattle, he and Junior found themselves locked in a home run duel. Frank had hit 28; Junior 32. Now both players were on pace to break Roger Maris's single-season record.

Would they do it? Since 1961, no one had come within eight homers of 61. In 1987, Eric Davis of the Reds set a National League record by hitting 19 homers before June 1 and finished the season with 37. In 1989, Kevin Mitchell of the San Francisco Giants hit 31 before the All-Star break in July, but just 16 more after that.

Junior didn't think he had much of a chance. "I'm still not a power hitter," he insisted. "Power hitters think about one thing when they step up to the plate, and that's hitting the ball out of the ballpark. I'm not thinking home run."

However, the public and the media were. The attention on Junior and Frank increased. People wondered if the two sluggers could handle the distractions and pressure.

HEAD TO HEAD

In 1994, Junior and Frank were gunning for the major league record for most home runs hit in one season (61). Junior had hit 40 and Frank 38 when the season ended on August 12 because of the baseball strike. Junior was on a pace to hit 58 homers during a normal 162-game schedule. Frank was on a pace to hit 54.

KEN GRIFFEY, JR.

When Roger Maris was trying to break Babe Ruth's record of 60 homers in a season, the pressure became so intense that his hair began to fall out!

Not to worry. The morning before the Mariners and White Sox would wrap up their three-game series, Junior hung out with Frank for a while. "We didn't talk about baseball," Junior told reporters. "We did check each other's hair, though. 'Yours falling out?' 'Naw, yours?'"

The two stars spent most of their time talking about their kids. "You talk about the pressure of hitting home runs," Junior laughed. "I'd rather go and try to hit a home run than change my son's diaper any day. I get one leg down, the other one goes up. I get both legs down and all of a sudden, he's sitting up."

In addition to the pressure, there was the looming possibility of a baseball strike. The team owners and players were locked in a nasty dispute about salaries. The owners wanted a "salary cap," or limit, on the amount of money each team could pay to *all* its players. The players insisted they would never agree to that.

Junior was asked if he was worried about a strike ruining his chance for the record. "I'm not even thinking about it," he said, referring to the record. "If it happens, it happens. If it doesn't, it wasn't meant to be."

On June 22, Junior hit his 31st homer of the season in a 12–3 win over the Angels in Anaheim. His shot broke Babe Ruth's record, set in 1928, of 30 homers by the end of June.

56 KEN GRIFFEY, JR.

The great home run derby continued into July. By the All-Star break, Junior was tied with Matt Williams of the Giants for the major league lead in homers. Each had 33. Frank Thomas was right behind with 32.

Of all the great performers that season, Junior was given the biggest salute by the fans. He received a record total of 6,079,688 All-Star votes. That was almost two million more than the record set by Rod Carew in 1977.

Junior showed what he was about at the All-Star home run-hitting contest on July 11th. *Sports Illustrated For Kids* magazine sent two reporters to Three Rivers Stadium, in Pittsburgh, where they were sitting in the open press box above the rightfield wall. Junior had them flinching and ducking for cover as he blasted shot after shot at them and over them.

In all, Junior put four blasts into the upper deck in rightfield. One of them traveled 512 feet! "I can't hit the ball harder than that," he said later.

Frank Thomas ended up hitting the longest shot that afternoon: a 519-foot drive off the face of the upper deck in left-centerfield. But Junior won the contest with a total of seven homers.

The Mariners opened the second half of the season in Seattle against the Yankees and were sunk when New York swept all four games. Two days later, the roof fell in, literally.

On July 19th, tiles attached to the ceiling of the

Kingdome started to fall into the stands.

"Maybe we can have a hard-hat promotional day," Seattle pitcher Randy Johnson joked.

Unfortunately, what had happened was no joke. The Kingdome was found to be so unsafe it had to be closed. The Mariners were forced to play their next 20 games on the road. Still, they won the last 6 of those 20, going 11 and 9, and climbed into third place, just two games behind first-place Texas.

Then on August 12th, the Mariners' and Junior's momentum all came to an abrupt halt. The major league baseball players went on strike. When the players and the owners couldn't resolve their differences, the season was cancelled for good on September 14th. For the first time in 90 years, there would be no playoffs and no World Series. And no one would know whether anyone would have broken the home run record. Matt Williams finished with 43 homers, Junior 40, and Frank Thomas 38.

Junior went home to play with Trey and spend more time with Melissa. "I'm on baby-sitting patrol," he told a reporter from *Newsday*. "I'm really frustrated because it was a good year for baseball to break through, as far as the records changing. Everyone wanted to see what was going to happen. Everyone wanted the whole year."

Junior summed up the 1994 season best when he said, "We picked a bad year to have a good year."

SAVING SEATTLE

The 1995 baseball season was a time when it seemed like anything could happen. The players' strike continued into spring training. Team owners tried to put together "replacement" teams made up of minor league players and former major leaguers, but few fans were interested in watching them. The big dispute was finally settled in court.

On April 1, a judge ruled that the owners had to pay players according to the rules of the agreement they had made before the strike. After 234 days, baseball was finally back.

The season finally began on April 26. Because it started later than usual, teams played 144 games instead of the usual 162. Right away it was clear that baseball had a lot of work to do to win back the many fans who were still angry about the strike. Attendance in most ballparks was down most of the year.

No team had more work to do than the Mariners. They needed a new stadium to replace the Kingdome, but fans in Seattle were tired of watching a losing team year

KEN GRIFFEY, JR.

after year. Most Mariner home games drew crowds of only 12,000 people. The Kingdome could hold more than 50,000. The owners of the team were losing money and the players were told they had to finish first in their division or else the Mariners would move to another city.

"Do you know what kind of pressure that is?" outfielder Jay Buhner told a reporter from *Sports Illustrated*. "Knowing that if you don't win, the team's going to skip town? Man, that's pressure."

Pressure or not, Junior was happy to get back to playing the game he loves. Returning to the field felt sweeter when he and his brother Craig played together in an exhibition game during the three-week training period before opening day.

During the first three weeks of the season, the Mariners stayed close to first place. Though Junior was batting .263, he led the team with 7 homers. There were signs that he was going to have another monster season. Then Junior broke two bones in his left wrist when he slammed into the centerfield fence after making a spectacular catch in a game against the Orioles on May 26.

Junior's injury was so severe he needed surgery. Doctors had to use a metal plate and seven screws to hold the broken bones together. Junior was not expected to play again until September.

Without their best player, the Mariners struggled to a 51–49 record by August 15. Their hopes of finishing first in their division were fading when Junior returned to the line-up that day, but the Mariners still lost. Things looked so bleak the players closed the locker room and held a meeting on August 24, before a game against the Yankees.

That night, Junior ignited his team by blasting a game-winning home run in the bottom of the ninth inning. The homer capped off a two-run rally the Mariners had staged when they were down to their final out. After that game, the Mariners were unstoppable

"That was the one that got us going," manager Lou Piniella told *Sports Illustrated*. "It wasn't just how we did it, but because Junior did it. We had him back."

The Mariners kept winning and winning and winning. After the final game of the regular season, they were tied with the Angels. The two teams met in a one-game playoff in Seattle on October 2. Mariner ace Randy Johnson pitched an overpowering game and Seattle buried the Angels, 9–1. The fans went crazy. The city of Seattle had caught Marinermania.

The Mariners flew to New York the next day to take on the Yankees in the division-playoff series. Junior belted a home run in each of the first two games, but the Mariners lost both. The second defeat became a real heartbreaker when Yankee catcher Jim Leyritz hit a game-winning homer in the bottom of the 15th inning.

"REFUSE TO LOSE!" signs were hung all over Seattle when the Mariners returned home for the next three

KEN GRIFFEY, JR.

games. They were one defeat away from being eliminated, but they took the slogan to heart. On October 6, Randy Johnson shut down New York, and Junior cracked another homer as the Mariners won, 7–4. The next night, Junior hit another blast as Seattle came back from being down 5–0 to win, 11–8. That set the stage for the incredible fifth and deciding game.

Many people feel the game was one of the most exciting ever played. Mariner fans on a flight from Denver, Colorado, to Seattle that night asked the pilot to keep them informed about the score. When the plane was over Washington State, the fans were able to listen to the play-

HEAD TO HEAD

Beating the Yankees in the 1995 American League division playoffs was sweet for Junior. He has never forgotten the occasion in 1983 when Yankee manager Billy Martin angrily ordered him out of the team's locker room. Junior was 14 at the time and his dad was a Yankee outfielder. Ken senior was upset, too. As for Frank, he doesn't carry a grudge against the Yankees but he hasn't made the team's life easy. Since 1991, Frank has hit .365 with nine homers and 36 RBIs in 48 games against New York.

by-play on the headphones because the plane could pick up the radio signal. And what a game it was. The Mariners were behind, 4–2, in the eighth inning when Junior set a playoff record by smacking his fifth home run of the series. The shot sparked a rally that let Seattle tie the score. And even though the Yankees scored a run in the top of the 11th, Seattle simply refused to lose.

The Kingdome was turned into a madhouse after Junior singled and then scored the winning run that night. The fans went crazy and TV cameras spotted Junior's smile shining from underneath the pile of happy teammates who buried him at home plate.

"I always wanted to be on the team that is jumping on one another, celebrating," Junior told reporters after the game.

Junior was asked if the victory had been his biggest baseball wish. "Third biggest," he replied. "Playing in the outfield with my father was first, then playing next to my brother in spring training."

Nine days later, the Cleveland Indians eliminated the Mariners in the league championship series, four games to two. Four days after that, Junior and his wife welcomed a daughter, Taryn, into the family.

The Mariners' magic season was over. Junior must wait for his next wish to come true: winning a World Series.

Winning the World Series would mean more to Junior than all the home runs he could ever hit. It would mean that he, too, is a champion.

"If the home runs help us win, fine," Junior told reporters after the big playoff game against the Yankees. "But they don't mean any more than anything else anyone does on our team to help out. Like the homer I hit in the eighth inning, I liked my single in the 11th more because it was part of the winning rally."

Junior has high hopes that the Mariners will be champions soon. Before the 1996 season began, he signed a new contract to play for Seattle through the year 2000. The contract will pay him $34 million, an average of $8.5 million per year. He is now the highest-paid player in the major leagues.

Junior knows that big responsibilities come with big paychecks. More than ever, people will expect him not only to lead the Mariners to a championship, but to be one of the greatest players of all time.

No matter what happens, Junior knows what he wants in the end. "When I'm done playing," he says, "I want people to say about me, 'He could flat-out play. He had fun while he played and I enjoyed watching him play.' That's all. I don't think about being the next Wille Mays. I just want to be the best player that I can be as Ken Griffey, Junior."

KEN GRIFFEY, JUNIOR'S CAREER STATS

YEAR	AVG.	G	AB	R	H	HR	RBI	SO	BB	SB
1989	.264	127	455	61	120	16	61	83	44	16
1990	.300	155	597	91	179	22	80	81	63	16
1991	.327	54	548	76	179	22	100	82	71	18
1992	.308	142	565	83	174	27	103	67	44	10
1993	.309	156	582	113	180	45	109	91	96	17
1994	.323	111	433	94	140	40	90	73	56	11
1995	.258	72	260	52	67	17	42	53	52	4
TOTAL	.302	917	3,440	570	1,039	189	585	530	426	92

In 1995, Junior's batting and fielding skills helped the Seattle Mariners make it to the playoffs for the first time and kept the team in Seattle.

Although Junior starred in football and baseball at Moeller High, in Cincinnati, Ohio, by his senior year, he had chosen baseball.

Tony Tomsic/Sports Illustrated

Junior's mom, Alberta (called "Birdie"), and dad, Ken senior, were proud when Junior became the first son of a major league player to be the number 1 draft choice.

In his first seven seasons in the majors,
Junior won six Gold Glove awards
for his outstanding fielding in centerfield.

Junior hit a home run and was named MVP of the 1992 All-Star Game. Twelve years earlier, his dad had homered and been named MVP of the All-Star Game!

Fans love Junior's fun-loving attitude toward baseball. He likes to clown around with his teammates, but he is very serious when it comes to hitting and fielding!

BOTH *KEN GRIFFEY, JUNIOR* AND *FRANK THOMAS* WERE VERY TALENTED IN MANY SPORTS AS KIDS — BUT THEIR PATHS TO THE MAJOR LEAGUES WERE VERY DIFFERENT.

WHILE *JUNIOR* WAS GROWING UP, HIS FATHER WAS A KEY PLAYER FOR THE *CINCINNATI REDS.* *JUNIOR* GOT TO HANG OUT IN *RIVERFRONT STADIUM* WITH THE KIDS OF OTHER PLAYERS.

FRANK GREW UP IN COLUMBUS, GEORGIA AND BOTH OF HIS PARENTS WORKED. FRANK AND HIS FRIENDS WOULD WALK A FEW MILES TO THE LOCAL BOYS CLUB AND PLAY SPORTS AFTER SCHOOL.

FOOTBALL WAS A MAJOR SPORT FOR BOTH KIDS. *JUNIOR* WAS A STAR WIDE RECEIVER ON THE STATE CHAMPION FOOTBALL TEAM AT *ARCHBISHOP MOELLER HIGH SCHOOL* IN CINCINNATI.

"I CAN'T BELIEVE HE'S THIS GOOD AT FOOTBALL, TOO!"

FRANK STARRED AS A PLACEKICKING TIGHT END, LOVED TO PLAY BASKETBALL, AND, AS A BASEBALL PLAYER, HE HIT .440 AND LED THE *COLUMBUS HIGH* TEAM TO A STATE TITLE.

"I NEVER HAVE TO WORRY ABOUT HIM. DAY OR NIGHT, HE IS SOMEWHERE WITH A BALL IN HIS HANDS!"

JUNIOR QUIT FOOTBALL HIS SENIOR YEAR IN HIGH SCHOOL BECAUSE HE DIDN'T LIKE TO BE TACKLED. WHEN HE WAS 17, THE *SEATTLE MARINERS* MADE *JUNIOR* THE FIRST PLAYER CHOSEN IN THE MAJOR LEAGUE DRAFT OF AMATEUR PLAYERS.

"THE SEATTLE MARINERS, WITH THE FIRST PICK, SELECT *KEN GRIFFEY, JUNIOR!*"

DESPITE HIS GREAT NUMBERS, *FRANK* WAS NOT DRAFTED OUT OF HIGH SCHOOL. SCOUTS FELT HE WAS GOING TO PLAY FOOTBALL, NOT BASEBALL. HE WAS SHATTERED, BUT ACCEPTED A FOOTBALL SCHOLARSHIP FROM *AUBURN*. IN HIS SOPHOMORE YEAR, HE DROPPED FOOTBALL AFTER INJURING HIS KNEE.

I AM MESSING UP MY BODY IN THIS SPORT!

JUNIOR SPENT ONLY TWO YEARS IN THE MINORS BEFORE HE WAS BROUGHT UP TO THE *MARINERS!* HE DOUBLED IN HIS FIRST BIG-LEAGUE AT BAT!

FRANK WAS FINALLY DRAFTED BY THE *CHICAGO WHITE SOX* AFTER HIS JUNIOR YEAR, WHEN HE HIT .403. AFTER 1½ SEASONS IN THE MINORS, HE MADE THE BIG CLUB ON AUGUST 3, 1990. IN THE LAST TWO MONTHS OF THE SEASON HE BATTED .330, HIT SEVEN HOME RUNS, AND HAD 31 RBIs.

"WHERE HAVE THEY BEEN KEEPING THIS KID? LOOK AT HIM SWING!"

FRANK AND JUNIOR ARE NOW TWO OF MAJOR LEAGUE BASEBALL'S BIGGEST STARS. ON THE ALL-STAR TEAM, THEY EVEN GET TO PLAY TOGETHER!

Tom DiPace

Over five full seasons with the Chicago White Sox, Frank has batted .323, averaged 35 home runs per season, and twice been named the American League's MVP!

When Frank was overlooked in the major league draft, he accepted a football scholarship to Auburn. He later quit football and starred on the baseball team.

After finishing eighth in the voting for League MVP in
1992, Frank worked on improving his fielding.
It paid off — he was the unanimous choice for MVP in
1993! He is one of only nine unanimous choices ever.

Frank is a smart — and terrifying — power hitter.
Pitchers often walk him because they are afraid
of the damage he can do with his bat.

For winning the home-run hitting contest at the 1995 All-Star Game, Frank was given this trophy and money for charity.

When it comes to head-to-head (or back-to-back) competition, Frank and Junior are friendly rivals who share the honor of being the best power hitters in the American League.

Walter Iooss Jr./Sports Illustrated

FRANK THOMAS'S CAREER STATS

YEAR	AVG.	G	AB	R	H	HR	RBI	SO	BB	SB
1990	.330	60	191	39	63	7	31	54	44	0
1991	.318	158	559	104	178	32	109	112	138	1
1992	.323	160	573	108	165	24	115	88	122	6
1993	.317	153	549	106	174	41	128	54	112	4
1994	.353	113	399	106	141	38	101	61	109	2
1995	.308	145	493	102	152	40	111	74	136	3
TOTAL	.323	789	2,764	565	893	182	595	443	661	16

choice for MVP in 1993. But he was asked by a reporter from *Sports Illustrated For Kids* if there was one moment on the playing field that really shows people what he is all about. Frank doesn't think he's had one yet.

"I've gotten a lot of big hits," Frank replied. "That thrill will always be there. People look at you like, 'You're not supposed to do that.' That's the type of player I am and the type of player I've always been. I love the big moment."

Hold on to your helmet. Frank's biggest moments are still to come.

motion. Imagine being as big and strong as he is and swinging at something that looks as inviting as a softball. No wonder Frank has already hit 182 homers in only five full seasons!

Frank has come a long way since the last two months of the 1990 season, when he made such an impressive major league debut. "I'm a much better player now," he says. "I try to build on things I've learned. I can't lay down on things I've done. I don't look back. You get yourself in trouble if you look back."

Like many great athletes, Frank is always setting new goals for himself. "I want to be one of those guys who make people say, 'Some of the things he did, I don't think can ever be done again,'" he says. "I want to be a Hall of Famer."

"Playing with Frank is like being part of history," Julio Franco told *Sports Illustrated,* in 1994.

Who knows? Maybe one day Frank will make history the same way Junior and his dad did in 1990 when they became the first father and son to play together in the major leagues. Sterling Thomas, who was born in the spring of 1992, is already showing signs of following in his famous dad's footsteps. "He's hitting the ball well now," Frank says. "He's got a great little stroke. I go home and all he wants to do is hit. I'm trying to teach him to switch-hit."

Frank's biggest thrill so far was being the unanimous

who goes to work and does a good job. Then you look at him on the field and you think, 'I guess he's pretty special.'"

Many baseball fans think so. That's why, when people argue about who is the best player in baseball, you'll always hear Frank's name included, whether the list of players being mentioned is long or short.

"I don't think I'm the best out there," Frank says, "but I think I work a little harder at what I do best than other guys. I'm so determined, so focused. I work throughout the year."

Frank works out during the winter and practices before games like many players do. But even when he's sitting in the dugout, he's always thinking of ways to make himself better.

"I sit on the bench and I'll watch a pitcher for the entire nine innings," Frank told sportswriter David Falkner of *The Sporting News*. "I'll try to know everything I can about how he delivers a baseball."

Watching the pitcher is one of the keys to Frank's amazing success as a hitter. Like Junior, Frank keeps things simple.

"I never guess [what kind of pitch will be thrown]," Frank told David Falkner. "What I'm trying to do is just see the ball come out of the pitcher's hand."

Frank has said that when he sees the ball well, it almost looks as if it were coming toward him in slow game on a close play at the plate. Then there was a great World Series matchup between the Indians and the Atlanta Braves, who won the championship in six games.

Almost lost and forgotten was the fact that Frank had had yet another great season. He made the All-Star team for the third time. He batted .308, with 40 homers, 111 RBIs, 102 runs scored, and 136 walks. That made him the first player in major league history to top .300, 20 homers, 100 RBIs, 100 runs, and 100 walks five seasons in a row.

That's an amazing accomplishment when you're only 27 years old, as Frank was. And keep in mind that most major leaguers reach their peak between the ages of 28 and 32.

Even Frank's family, the people who don't think of him as a superstar, is impressed. "We all know what he does and how talented he is," Elise said, "and we're all proud of him the same way we'd be proud of any husband

HEAD TO HEAD

Both Frank and Junior have done a lot in a short time. Frank, 28, is already the only major leaguer ever to top .300, 20 homers, 100 RBIs, 100 runs scored, and 100 walks in five consecutive seasons. Junior, 26, is the youngest player ever to start in five All-Star Games.

After the contest, Frank was presented with a special trophy, which he later put next to his two MVP trophies in a display case at home. "The MVP is special, but fans want to see some long home runs, so I made sure to hit some very far," Frank told reporters. "It's something I'm very proud of. We had some fun and that's what this is all about."

Frank had more fun the next night in the All-Star Game. Batting in the bottom of the fourth inning, he cracked a two-run homer off National League pitcher John Smiley. The shot gave the American League a 2–0 lead before the National League rallied to win the game, 3–2.

"He's amazing," Red Sox slugger Mo Vaughn told reporters. "When he gets a pitch that he can handle, he doesn't miss."

The All-Star Game helped get fans back into baseball. During the early part of the season, many people were still mad about the strike, so attendance at games was down. But as the summer went along, the excitement, and the fans, started to return.

The biggest story of the season was the performance by Cal Ripken, Junior of the Orioles. On September 6, Cal broke Lou Gehrig's all-time major league playing record of 2,130 games in a row. The playoffs were exciting, too, especially the series between the Mariners and the Yankees. Ken Griffey, Junior, set a playoff record by hitting five home runs in five games and scored the winning run in the final scheduled to play 144 regular season games instead of 162.

Some players had a hard time getting back into shape. Frank didn't. He'd been working out all winter, as usual, and was ready to go. Unfortunately, the rest of the White Sox were not.

Chicago had a miserable season. Pitcher Jack McDowell had been traded to the Yankees during the winter and the pitching staff collapsed. The offense was hurt when Julio Franco left to play in Japan. The defense was shaky, too. The Sox made 21 errors in their first six games!

On June 2, manager Gene Lamont was fired and replaced by Terry Bevington. It didn't help. The Sox were quickly buried in the American League Central by the powerhouse Cleveland Indians, who went on to win 100 games and lose only 44. By the All-Star break, in mid-July, the Sox were 17½ games behind.

The All-Star Game was held on July 11 at The Ballpark, in Arlington, Texas. It was one of the high points of the season for Frank.

The day before the game, Frank put on a mind-blowing power show in the All-Star home run-hitting contest. Junior, his friendly rival, missed the game because he had broken his wrist, so Frank's toughest competitor was Albert Belle of the Indians. Albert was on his way to hitting 50 homers that season. Frank blew him away by winning the contest with 15 big blasts. The average distance of each one was 432.5 feet. The longest one traveled 470 feet.

LOVING THE BIG MOMENTS

The 1995 season was growing near and it looked as if Frank was going to have a *really* long layoff. Team owners weren't interested in ending the strike. Instead, they were putting together teams of replacement players. Many people feared that if fans did not watch "replacement ball," the owners would lose so much money that major league baseball with regular players would not be seen again until 1996 or beyond.

When small crowds showed up for replacement games during spring training, the worst was about to happen. Luckily, the strike was settled in a court of law. On April 1, a judge ruled that the owners had to pay the players according to the rules of the agreement they had made before the strike. The next day, the two sides agreed. Baseball was back.

Everyone had to scramble to get ready. It was decided that the regular season would start on April 26, three weeks later than usual. Spring training would be shorter. And because of the delay caused by the strike, teams were used his time off to start thinking about his future. In October, he started Big Hurt Enterprises to handle his fan mail, marketing deals, and charity projects.

"Sports marketing is where I want to be when I retire," he says. "Whenever I decide to get out of this game, I've already got a successful business set up."

Life without baseball felt strange for Frank and his family. "We have a Sox calendar on the kitchen counter," Elise Thomas told *USA Today*. "Every time I see it, I wonder who we'd be playing and who would be winning. It would have been nice to see what could have been."

"This is the year I thought we had a chance to win the World Series," Frank said. "This is the time when the total focus is on baseball. The whole world is watching. It's real different being at home, doing nothing. It's sad."

The bright side was that Frank got to spend more time with his kids. "Most of the time, I wouldn't see the kids unless they were awake late at night," he said. "Now it's like being a normal father. I'm home. I wake up with the kids. It's been fun."

Frank looked forward to the day when the strike would be over and baseball would return.

"I guess we'll be well-rested when we come back," he said. "I think you'll see a higher level of performance when the guys come back, because everyone wants to do well after such a long layoff."

And no one wanted to do well more than Frank.

Matt Williams was ahead with 43 homers, Junior was second with 40, and Frank third with 38. No one would ever know if any of them would have broken Roger Maris's record. Frank also lost his chance for that year to win the Triple Crown and break three records that had been set by Babe Ruth: most walks (170), total bases (457), and runs scored (177).

Frank's totals were dazzling if you consider that he only played 113 games instead of the normal 162. He batted .353, with 38 homers, 101 RBIs, 106 runs, 109 walks, and had a .487 on-base percentage. Try to imagine how high those totals would have been if Frank had been able to play another 49 games!

On October 26, Frank became only the 11th player ever to win back-to-back MVP awards. He was the first American League player to do it since Roger Maris in 1960 and 1961. But unlike the year before, Frank was not a unanimous choice. Junior received three first-place votes from the writers.

How valuable was Frank to his team? The Sox had a 27–9 record in games in which he homered, a 45–17 record in games in which he drove in a run, and a 51–21 record when he scored a run.

"I'm very happy," Frank told reporters, "but it's kind of bittersweet, too. Individual awards don't mean anything if you don't win as a team."

Frank missed not being able to play, but he wisely

From June 5 to 20, the Sox had lost 12 of 15 games and fallen six games behind the Indians. The Sox rallied to win their last six games before the All-Star break, and both teams entered the second half of the season tied for first, with 52–34 records.

"We've got our work cut out for us in the second half," Frank told reporters.

Frank was right. The two teams split the series and another four games in Cleveland four days later. An exciting pennant race was brewing.

By July 25, the home run race was really cooking. Matt Williams and Junior were tied with 36 each. Frank had 35, but was more proud of his .371 batting average.

"I don't really care about the home run title," Frank told *Sports Illustrated*, "because people will say, 'Dang. Six-five, 275 pounds. He's supposed to win that.' I'd rather have the batting title. Guys my size aren't supposed to win that."

Unfortunately, Frank and his teammates weren't going to win anything. The Sox were in first place with a 67–46 record on August 12 when the major league players went on strike. There was a bit of hope during the next few weeks that the strike would be settled and the season would resume. But on September 14, the team owners canceled all the remaining games, including the playoffs and the World Series.

The Great Home Run Derby had been called off.

FRANK THOMAS 53

know how big his career year is," Mr. Lamont said.

Frank wasn't paying too much attention to winning titles or breaking records. The Sox were about to play an important four-game series at home against the Indians.

HEAD TO HEAD

Only 11 players in modern big-league history have won the Triple Crown by leading their league in batting average, home runs, and RBIs in the same season. Many people think Frank's name will appear on this list before his career is over.

Player	Year	Team	Avg.	HRs	RBIs
Ty Cobb	1909	Tigers	.377	9	115
H. Zimmerman	1912	Cubs	.372	14	98
Rogers Hornsby	1922	Cards	.401	42	152
	1925	Cards	.403	39	143
Chuck Klein	1933	Phillies	.368	28	120
Jimmie Foxx	1933	A's	.356	48	163
Lou Gehrig	1934	Yankees	.363	49	165
Ducky Medwick	1937	Cards	.374	31	154
Ted Williams	1942	Red Sox	.356	36	137
	1947	Red Sox	.343	32	114
Mickey Mantle	1956	Yankees	.353	52	130
Frank Robinson	1966	Orioles	.316	49	122
Carl Yastrzemski	1967	Red Sox	.326	44	121

of them into the upper deck where only 11 homers had landed since 1970. One of Junior's shots traveled 512 feet! Junior won the contest, but Frank hit the longest blast of the contest. It was a monster drive off the face of the upper deck in left-center, 519 feet away.

Frank didn't mind losing to his friend. "Junior is a pure home run hitter," Frank explained. "I've been a line-drive hitter all my life."

Frank and Junior both played well in the All-Star Game on July 12. Frank had two hits in two times at bat and drove in a run with a single in the first inning. Junior was two-for-three, with an RBI, but the National League won the game, 8–7.

The Great Home Run Derby continued when the regular season resumed on July 14. Besides going for the home run record, Frank also had a shot at winning the "Triple Crown," which is what it's called when a player leads the league in batting, homers, and RBIs. The last player to win it was Carl Yastrzemski of the Boston Red Sox, in 1967.

Frank was leading the American League in batting with a .383 average, and was second in homers with 32 and RBIs with 78, only three behind leader Kirby Puckett of the Twins.

White Sox Manager Gene Lamont was asked by a reporter if 1994 was going to be the biggest season of Frank's career. "I'd call it a career year, except I don't received. By the final month of the 1961 season, his hair was falling out because of the stress.

Frank wasn't distracted by all the hoopla. Junior was getting most of the attention and Frank saw that as an advantage. "He's deflecting attention away from me, which is good," he told reporter Claire Smith of *The New York Times*. "I'm having the best year of my career so far. And I'm having fun just going out and doing what I'm doing."

Frank was asked if he and Junior were competing against each other in a race for the home run record. "There's competition, friendly competition," Frank replied. "And it's more than just me and Ken. It's all of us. I don't think it's going to get too crazy, because we all know there's going to be a player strike."

Junior cracked homer number 32 the next night in a 6–2 loss to the Sox. The home run went 400 feet and Frank wasn't the least bit surprised. "He said he was going to go deep," he said after the game. "He's definitely in a groove. He's a natural."

Frank and Junior both made the American League All-Star team. There was a lot of excitement when they competed in a home run-hitting contest the day before the All-Star Game. At the time, Junior was tied with Matt Williams for the major league lead in homers with 33. Frank was right behind them with 32.

The crowd in Pittsburgh's Three Rivers Stadium gasped and cheered as Junior walloped seven homers, five derby, as the race to beat Roger's record was called. The White Sox and Mariners met in Seattle on June 23rd. Junior had already broken Babe Ruth's record of 30 homers by the end of June and was leading the majors with 31. Frank was right behind with 28. Matt Williams of the San Francisco Giants had 27.

The two sluggers met by the batting cage before the game. "We didn't talk about baseball," Junior told reporters. "We just talked about his daughter and my son getting married."

"We'll build a super athlete!" Frank had said.

Frank and Junior also joked about their hair falling out. That actually happened to Roger Maris in 1961. The closer he came to breaking Babe Ruth's record of 60 homers, set in 1927, the more pressure and attention Roger

HEAD TO HEAD

Frank and Junior were the American League's top two home run hitters in 1994. Junior hit 40 and Frank 38. They also squared off in a homer-hitting contest before the All-Star Game, in July. Junior hit the most home runs (7) but Frank hit the longest blast (519 feet). Junior has been an All-Star six times. Frank has been chosen three times.

"With the way he's hitting, he should be in another league — like on Mars," Frank told reporter Mel Antonen of *USA Today*. "I like his style. He's having fun. He's playing like he did on the playground — swinging hard and the balls are going far."

Frank wasn't doing too poorly himself. By the end of May, he was batting .374, with 20 homers and 48 RBIs. And he was hitting the ball incredibly hard.

On May 30, the Sox played the Yankees in New York. In the fourth inning, Frank blistered a ball that hit Yankee pitcher Jim Abbott in the left thigh. Jim was rattled and gave up a three-run homer two batters later as the Sox went on to win, 7–2.

After the game, Jim had a red bruise shaped like a baseball on his thigh. "Frank is as tough a batter as there is in the American League," Jim told reporters. "He's phenomenally strong."

"He's in a groove where if he gets his pitch, he doesn't miss it," Sox manager Gene Lamont said.

The Sox were in a groove, too. From May 15 to 28, they won 10 of their 11 games to grab a four-game lead in the American League Central.

Meanwhile, Frank and Junior kept bashing away. A lot was written and said about how both had a chance to break the major league record of 61 home runs in a season that had been set by Roger Maris of the Yankees in 1961.

Reporters were closely following this great home run

or limit, on the amount of money each team could pay to all its players. The players refused this proposal. Discussions were held during the next few months, but the owners and players could not find a way to settle their differences.

By spring training, there was a good chance the players would go on strike sometime that season. Frank didn't waste time worrying. He stayed focused and worked hard to prepare for the upcoming season.

Frank's goal was to get off to a good start. In the past three seasons, he had hit only .265 during the month of April. He knew he could do better, so he spent extra time working on his batting with batting coach Hriniak.

The effort was worth it. In his first 23 games, Frank batted .295, with 8 homers and 20 RBIs. The Sox started well, too. The team's offense was boosted by new designated hitter Julio Franco (who ended up hitting 20 homers and driving in 98 runs over the course of the season). Pitcher Wilson Alvarez won his first eight starts and the Sox grabbed first place in early May.

It didn't take long before people around the country noticed that home runs were flying out of ballparks in record numbers. More than 30 players hit two homers in a game the first month of the season. By May 23, Ken Griffey, Junior, had broken Mickey Mantle's major league record for most homers (20) hit in the first two months of the season.

Frank was impressed by how well Junior was doing.

THE GREAT HOME RUN DERBY

The spring of 1994 was a time of new beginnings. The major leagues were celebrating the 125th year of professional baseball. Each league was divided into three divisions instead of two. The White Sox were now in the American League Central with the Cleveland Indians, Kansas City Royals, Milwaukee Brewers, and Minnesota Twins. A new playoff format had been created. The winner of each division and the team with the best second-place record would qualify for postseason play.

The Thomas family enjoyed a new beginning of their own, on March 23, when Elise gave birth to a baby girl, Sloan Alexandra.

All in all, 1994 looked like it was going to be a great year, though dark clouds were gathering off the field. The major league owners were complaining that player salaries were too high and that as many as 19 of the 28 big-league teams were losing money. The owners wanted a "salary cap,"

Frank's totals for the season were his best so far: a .317 batting average, 41 homers, 128 RBIs, 106 runs scored, and 112 walks. More important, he had really helped his team. Of his 41 homers, 22 of them had either tied the score or put the Sox ahead.

The icing on the MVP cake came when the other American League players chose Frank as their player of the year. "I feel more excited about this award than I would winning one voted by the media," Frank told writer Michael Kinsley of *The Sporting News*. "When you've got other players voting and they tell you you deserve it, it makes you step back for a second."

Winning MVP awards was definitely rewarding for Frank. It was something he could get into the habit of doing.

McDowell got shelled again and the Sox lost, 5–3, in Game 5. It was back to Chicago and a do-or-die situation. One more loss and the Sox would be eliminated.

Game 6 turned out to be the day broadcaster Ken Harrelson had predicted would come. The Blue Jays actually walked Frank with the bases loaded! The walk forced in a run to tie the score at 2–2 in the third inning, but it was a smart move. The other Chicago hitters failed to drive in any more runs. The Sox scored only once more the rest of the game and lost, 6–3.

Frank did not reach his goal of winning the American League pennant, but he did receive a couple of very nice consolation prizes.

On November 10, Frank got a phone call from Jack Lang, the director of the Baseball Writers Association of America. "I answered on the first ring," Frank later told reporter Chuck Johnson of *USA Today*. "I was nervous."

Mr. Lang told Frank that he had been chosen the American League MVP. Not only that, Frank had received first-place votes from all 28 writers who chose the winner. In the 63-year history of the MVP award, only nine other players had ever been unanimous winners. Only two other White Sox (Hall of Famer Nellie Fox in 1959 and Dick Allen in 1972) had ever won the award.

Frank thought about all the good young players he had been selected over that season and said, "That makes winning this very special."

pitcher Jerry DiPoto refused to give him anything good to hit. Frank walked on five pitches and angrily threw his batting helmet into the dugout when the inning ended. He was angry at being denied the chance to win the title, even though Chicago was now on its way to the playoffs. As it turned out, the walk was a bad sign of things to come.

The White Sox opened the playoffs at home against Toronto on October 5. Special guest Michael Jordan threw out the first ball. Then the crowd of 46,246 fans watched in frustration as Toronto pitcher Juan Guzman walked Frank three times. The Sox received 10 walks in all, but only scored three runs. Meanwhile, Jack McDowell, a 22-game winner that season, was rattled for 13 hits and 7 runs. Chicago lost, 7–3.

Things did not go any better the next day. Toronto ace Dave Stewart shut down Chicago, 3–1. The Sox weren't hitting and were shaky in the field. Frank had to be the designated hitter because his arm was still sore. Dan Pasqua, his replacement at first base, made one of Chicago's two errors in the game.

The Sox were in a big hole when the series moved to Toronto, but they fought back to win the next two games. Frank returned to first base for Game 3 and drove in one of Chicago's six runs. The next day, he homered as the Sox won, 7–4.

Just when things were starting to look brighter, Jack

"There's hits and there's *hits*," sportswriter Bob Ryan wrote in *The Boston Globe*. "When Thomas happens to hit 14 of his first 40 homers in the first inning, that means he has already put his team in position to win more than anyone else in baseball."

Frank thought he deserved the award, but new goals had become more important. "People talk about MVP," Frank told sportswriter Murray Chass of *The New York Times*. "That's a secondary thing for me this year. My first is winning the A.L. West and then the pennant."

Frank got his first wish on September 27, when the Sox beat the Mariners, 4–2, to clinch first place. It was Chicago's first division title in 10 years.

After the Sox celebrated, Frank rested for the next five games. He had banged his left forearm on a fence while chasing a pop fly on September 19, and his muscles were still sore and swollen. White Sox manager Gene Lamont wanted to be sure his star slugger was healthy for the upcoming playoffs against Toronto.

Despite the injury and his need for rest, Frank was allowed to play in the last regular season game because he had a shot at winning the RBI title. He drove in two runs against Cleveland during the first six innings and then came up in the eighth with a runner on first. If Frank could drive him in, he would be tied with Cleveland's Albert Belle, who had 129 RBIs.

Frank really wanted to win the RBI title, but Indian

many people were saying he deserved to be MVP. Other contenders for the award were first baseman John Olerud of the Toronto Blue Jays and Ken Griffey, Junior.

John was trying to become the first player to bat .400 or higher in a season since Ted Williams did it in 1941. Junior had tied a major league record by hitting homers in eight consecutive games and was on his way to final totals of 45 homers, 109 RBIs, and a .309 batting average.

So who was more valuable to their team?

People who favored John argued that batting .400 was very rare and his team was going to finish first in the American League East. Junior's fans argued that he should be MVP because he was having his best season ever. Frank's fans pointed out that his numbers were as good as Junior's, but Junior's team was struggling. The Sox were in first place, just like the Blue Jays, but Toronto had more good hitters than Chicago. Frank was his team's only big gun.

HEAD TO HEAD

Frank won his first American League MVP award in 1993. The award was partly due to the hard work he had done to improve his fielding at first base. Although he has improved, he has still never won a Gold Glove award for fielding excellence. Junior has won five.

Yankees intentionally walked Frank in the first inning, even though there was already a runner on second base and only one out. The Sox went on to win, 4–2.

"We didn't want to let him hurt us with a mistake [a good pitch to hit]," Yankee catcher Mike Stanley later explained to reporters. "He'll kill your mistakes."

Frank killed his share of Yankee mistakes that season. When the two teams met again a week later for a three-game series in New York, Frank hit a homer and drove in the winning run in each of the first two games. His second homer broke the White Sox single-season team record of 38 home runs that had been set by Dick Allen in 1972 and tied by Carlton Fisk in 1985.

"I'm happy and I'm very fortunate," Frank told reporters. "I've hit my share of home runs and most of them haven't been cheap. So I'm very proud inside."

After the game, a group of Yankees sat in their clubhouse and tried to figure out how in the world to pitch to Frank and still keep the ball in the park. "We should just walk him every time up. It can't get any worse," one Yankee pitcher said.

Chicago broadcaster Ken Harrelson predicted that someday, a team would intentionally walk Frank with the bases loaded. "And when they do, I will stand up and applaud them for their intelligence," Ken said. "In my 30 years in this game, I have never seen anyone like him."

By mid-September, Frank had hit 40 homers and

homer. It was one of 15 homers he hit in the first inning of games that season. "I call them my school bells," Frank told *Sports Illustrated*. "The offense is in session."

The offense was still in session in the seventh inning when Frank cracked another two-run shot as the White Sox beat the Orioles, 11–5.

The All-Star Game was played at Camden Yards, in Baltimore, on July 13. Frank did not compete in the popular home run-hitting contest that takes place the day before. He kept telling reporters he wasn't a home run hitter. "Nothing puts a smile on my face like a high average and RBIs," Frank said. He got only one at-bat in the All-Star Game, singling as a pinch-hitter in the eighth inning as the American League won easily, 9–3.

After the regular season resumed, Frank carried the Sox through a tight race with the Texas Rangers by batting .336, with 21 homers and 60 RBIs in Chicago's last 76 games. He was absolutely amazing almost every day.

On August 23, the White Sox played at home against the Yankees. In the 10th inning, Frank hit a line drive over the head of Yankee reliever Steve Farr. Batting coach Walt Hriniak was sure the ball would be caught by the centerfielder, but it kept rising and going and going . . .

"If it hadn't hit the seats, it might still be going," Coach Hriniak later told a reporter from *Sports Illustrated*.

The White Sox lost that game, but the next night, the

commendable, considering the offensive numbers he put up the year before."

Frank's hard work paid off. He later told a reporter that one of his favorite moments that season was not when he hit a home run or got a game-winning hit, it was a great defensive play he made at first base. "I dove to my right, then threw home to get the runner," he said. "I don't think I could have made that play before this year."

The White Sox were a good team that had strong pitching, led by ace Jack McDowell. They had plenty of speed with outfielders Tim Raines and Lance Johnson, but they still needed a super year from Frank. He was their only real power hitter. Of course, some good defensive play from him wouldn't hurt, either.

Frank had a red hot first half of the season. He batted .302, with 20 homers and 68 RBIs. He led the Sox into first place by mid-July. This time, he was not overlooked when it came time to pick players for the 1993 All-Star team.

Oddly, Frank went into a little slump after learning he had been chosen as an American League All-Star for the first time in his career. He failed to get a hit in nine straight at-bats and was razzed by his teammates. "They were all over me," Frank told a reporter from *USA Today*. "They try to get on my nerves. They know I play better when I'm mad."

In the final game before the All-Star break, mad Frank hit the fourth pitch of the first inning for a two-run

MVP, HANDS DOWN

Great athletes in every sport always try to make themselves more complete. Michael Jordan, for example, is a dazzling scorer who practiced hard to improve his defense and passing. Frank is one of baseball's most feared hitters, but that reputation didn't satisfy him.

"I got a little tired of hearing, 'Yeah, but he can't field,'" Frank says.

During spring training in 1993, Frank worked like mad to become a better first baseman. He was driven by his desire to win the league's MVP award. He had finished eighth in the voting by baseball writers the season before, leaving him disappointed. He knew that if he could help his team more in the field, he would be an even more valuable player.

Each morning, Frank arrived at Chicago's training camp, in Sarasota, at 7:30 A.M. "He busted his butt," White Sox general manager Ron Schueler told *USA Today* newspaper. "He'd work until the pitchers got there at ten o'clock, and then get involved in infield drills. That's stresses to me is keeping my head down [when I swing]. You need a chance to see the baseball, and he makes sure I do that."

Thanks to some tips from Walt, Frank had another monster season. He even had a 19-game hitting streak. Frank finished with a .323 batting average, 24 homers, 115 RBIs, 122 walks, and only 88 strikeouts. Unfortunately, the Sox didn't take advantage of his booming bat. Injuries and poor pitching caused Chicago to finish third again.

Frank's performance made him only the eighth player in modern major league history to bat .300 or higher with 20 or more homers, 100 or more RBIs, 100 or more runs scored, and 100 or more walks in consecutive seasons. The other seven players are all in the Hall of Fame: Babe Ruth, Lou Gehrig, Ted Williams, Stan Musial, Jimmie Foxx, Mel Ott, and Hank Greenberg.

That's a pretty impressive list to be on, and an even better season for Frank was still to come.

it over and over again. I think he can do it. He's not afraid of being good. He works hard."

By the beginning of spring training in 1992, the baseball world had discovered just how good Frank is. Sportswriters were comparing him to such Hall of Fame sluggers as Babe Ruth and Ted Williams.

Other people wondered if Frank was really that good.

The White Sox thought so. Before spring training, they gave him a new three-year contract for which he would be paid about four million dollars. Frank understood that fans expect bigger things when a player receives big money.

"That's all right," he told reporter Bob Ryan of the *The Boston Globe*. "I want people to expect greatness from me. After all, I expect it from myself."

During spring training, Frank kept working to perfect his hitting. One of his goals was to cut down on his strikeouts. He had whiffed 112 times during the 1991 season, and he thought that total was too high.

Other people thought Frank's walk total was too high. He and Coach Hriniak were criticized because Frank seemed to be wasting his power. The critics said he should swing more often. If he did, he would surely hit more home runs. He would also strike out more, but that wouldn't matter, they said.

"I disagree strongly," Frank told writer Bob Ryan. "Walt stresses discipline. He can help any hitter. What he

FRANK THOMAS 35

asked Frank if he was thinking about the award. "Yeah, I think about it," Frank said. But he also went on to point out, "I've got to stay focused, stay hungry, and we've got to keep winning."

Unfortunately, the Sox didn't keep winning. After closing to within one game of the Twins, Chicago lost 15 of their next 17 games and fell into third place, nine games behind. They ended up finishing second with an 87–75 record, eight games back.

Failing to win a division title could not erase the great year Frank had. He finished his first full season ranked in the league's Top 10 in batting average (.318), home runs (32), RBIs (109), and walks (138). He also led the major leagues with a .453 on-base percentage. That means Frank got on base almost every other time he went to bat.

Frank's fine performance made him a worthy choice for MVP, but he finished third behind shortstop Cal Ripken, Junior, of the Orioles and first baseman Cecil Fielder of the Tigers in the voting by baseball writers.

Back in Columbus, Frank's biggest fan was still happy. "He's made me prouder than a father could be," Frank senior told *Sports Illustrated*.

Batting coach Walt Hriniak thought Frank would make his dad even prouder in coming seasons. "He's young and has a long way to go, but he has done it so far," Walt told reporters. "The true test of a great performer is doing player in six years to drive in 100 runs.

"He has amazed everyone," manager Jeff Torborg told reporters. "He carried us through the first six weeks of the season when some other guys were struggling."

As well as Frank played, the White Sox struggled to win as a team. By the break for the All-Star Game in mid-July, they were in fourth place with a 43–37 record. Frank wasn't chosen to play on the American League All-Star Team, but he didn't mind. He wanted to be with Elise, who gave birth to their son, Sterling, the day before the game.

"I watched the game in the hospital, holding him in my arms," Frank says.

On July 25, the Sox finally caught fire and won 15 of their next 17 games. As usual, Frank and his big bat were in the thick of the action.

On July 30 at the SkyDome, in Toronto, Blue Jay pitcher Bob McDonald intentionally walked Robin Ventura so he could face Frank instead. Big mistake. The score was tied, 6–6, in the seventh inning. Frank blasted a two-run homer and the White Sox won, 8–7.

By August 11, the Sox were in second place, only one game behind the Minnesota Twins. Frank kept hitting and hitting and hitting. He was named the American League Player of the Month for August, after batting .371, with 8 homers, 27 RBIs, and 24 walks.

Many people thought Frank had a great chance to win the league's Most Valuable Player award. A reporter

On June 24 at Comiskey Park, Frank belted a game-winning grand slam in the eighth inning against the Seattle Mariners. The crowd of 42,552 roared as he circled the bases. "Probably the most exciting moment of my career," Frank told reporters after the game. "I even showed emotion. I threw my fist in the air."

Frank's dad often had his hand in the air, too. Mr. Thomas didn't like to fly, so he hadn't seen Frank play for the Sox in person, but he always watched on TV back home in Columbus. Whenever Frank was up, Mr. Thomas pretended he was with his son. He would close his eyes slightly, hold his right arm out straight, and open his hand wide. "When Frank is at the plate, I feel like I'm at the plate," he explained to a reporter from *Sports Illustrated*.

During Chicago's first 90 games, Frank hit .304, with 16 homers, and was leading the league with 79 walks. His 61 RBIs gave him a chance to become the first White Sox

HEAD TO HEAD

Frank played his first full season with Chicago in 1991. On April 22, 1991, he became the first White Sox player to hit a home run in the new Comiskey Park, which had opened three days earlier. That season was also the last for Ken Griffey, Senior, who retired that fall.

old Comiskey Park had been torn down) and new black-and-silver uniforms. "I love the look," Frank told a reporter.

Manager Jeff Torborg was asked if he thought Frank would continue to play as well as he had after joining the White Sox the summer before. "You can hope," Jeff replied, "but you can't expect him to do what he did in two months the previous year."

Jeff was happy to learn that he could expect big things from Frank almost every day. Batting third in the lineup, behind speedy outfielder Tim Raines and hot-hitting third baseman Robin Ventura, Frank had plenty of chances to drive in runs — and did.

The White Sox got off to a great start by winning their first six games. On April 22, Frank hit the first home run by a White Sox player in the new Comiskey Park as Chicago beat Baltimore, 8–7. During the first three months of the season, there were three games in which he drove in five runs.

White Sox TV broadcaster Ken Harrelson marveled at how Frank didn't just hit the ball, he punished it. So Ken started calling Frank "The Big Hurt" because of the way he hurt the ball and injured the confidence of pitchers he faced.

Sportswriters noticed how serious and scary Frank looked whenever he stood in the batter's box. He often stared at the pitcher and slowly moved the barrel of his bat in little circles. He looked like a coiled cobra ready to strike.

Sometimes, another side of Frank would come out.

was at the restaurant with her cousin. "He bumped into me."

Frank and Elise liked each other right away. That Frank is black and Elise is white never bothered them. "People might think there would be some cultural difficulties," Elise once told *Sports Illustrated*, "but when you come from two loving families, it's pretty easy. Besides, we had baseball in common."

Elise has baseball in her blood. Silver Stadium, the home of the minor league Rochester Red Wings, in Rochester, New York, is named after Elise's great-uncle Maury.

By the end of spring training, Frank was ready to show what he could do. "It's time to perform," he said. "People are saying this and that about what Frank Thomas can do. The truth is, I haven't done anything yet. I want to do things that haven't been done."

Just in case he got a big head from all the glowing praise he received from fans and the media, Frank printed "D.B.T.H." in black marker on a piece of white tape and stuck it to the top of his locker. The letters stood for "Don't Believe The Hype." It was Frank's way of warning himself that if he started to believe that greatness comes easily, he might stop working hard.

The beginning of the season was a time of great hope and excitement for the White Sox. The team was expected to win their division. They had a brand new ballpark (the

4

THE BIG HURT

Frank spent the month of January 1991 in Los Angeles working out with sluggers Darryl Strawberry and Eric Davis of the Dodgers. Eric and Darryl were two of baseball's biggest stars, and they saw that Frank was a new star about to rise.

"Awesome. Totally," Eric told *Sports Illustrated*. "You don't see many big guys with the bat speed and agility he has. The only thing that can stop Frank from having success is Frank."

During spring training, Frank worked with Walt Hriniak, one of the best batting coaches in the majors. Walt helped Frank improve his ability to hit balls to all areas of the field.

Frank also improved another area of his life when he met Elise Silver, who would become his wife. They met after Frank drove a hungry teammate to a restaurant in Sarasota. "We looked like a couple of bums," Frank told *Sports Illustrated*.

"I guess you could say we met cute," says Elise, who

a hit, but the next day he drove in the winning run with a triple.

"We immediately pushed him into the heat of the pennant race," White Sox manager Jeff Torborg explained. "He responded right away."

Frank got at least one hit in 45 of the 60 games he played for the White Sox that season. He went on a 13-game hitting streak from September 17 to 30, and finished with a .330 batting average, 7 homers, and 31 RBIs. Most of all, Frank helped the White Sox put up a good fight. Still, the Sox finished second to the A's.

There was no question he was in the big leagues to stay. "You could see it right away," White Sox batting coach Walt Hriniak told reporters. "The size he has, the way the ball goes off his bat. He has a chance to be a great offensive player."

Frank's road to the big leagues had been full of hard work and disappointment. Now the fun was beginning.

"I knew that was where I did not want to be, so I went out and tried to do some things in that league that had never been done," he says. "I took that league by storm."

Indeed, he did. In 109 games for the Barons, Frank batted .323, with 18 homers, 71 RBIs, and a league-leading 112 walks. Once again, pitchers were trying not to give him anything to hit. Once again, Frank got frustrated with this strategy as he had in college. But he stayed patient and kept producing big numbers.

Meanwhile, the White Sox, who had finished last the season before, were battling the Oakland A's for first place in the American League West division. Fans in Chicago had heard about the great things Frank was doing in Birmingham. They wondered why he hadn't been called up to the majors. Chicago had three first basemen — Ron Kittle, Carlos Martinez, and Greg Walker — and none of them were playing well. Didn't the White Sox need a good young slugger like Frank?

Frank thought so. "I was going night after night, hitting home run after home run," he told *Sports Illustrated*. "I thought, 'Why can't the big-league team use this?' It had no one who could produce at first base. I didn't understand that. I was stepping on the gas as much as possible."

Finally, Frank was rewarded with a promotion to the White Sox. He played his first big-league game on August 2, 1990, against the Brewers in Milwaukee. Frank failed to get would make it in less than a year when he put on a show at the White Sox spring-training camp in 1990.

In seven exhibition games, Frank blistered the baseball for a .529 average, with 2 homers and 7 RBIs. He believed he would make the team, but the White Sox thought he should spend more time in the minors. Why? He needed to work on his fielding at first base.

Frank was very unhappy when he learned he was being sent to the Birmingham Barons of the AA Southern League. Before reporting to the team, Frank drove home to Columbus and had a talk with his dad.

"He was hurt," Mr. Thomas told *Sports Illustrated*. "Really hurt. But he was dedicated to working hard and being ready."

"He's got some work to do," Birmingham Baron manager Ken Berry told reporters early in the season. "Frank's going to have to keep working on his defense. I don't think he received a lot of knowledge of fielding in college. Back there it was just 'Take the bat and hit the ball.' So it may take awhile."

It took Frank most of the season. He made nine errors in his first 57 games, yet he improved steadily.

Playing for Birmingham wasn't easy. The Barons made their players work out with weights two or three times a week and take extra hitting and fielding practice before games. But Frank met the challenge because he was absolutely determined to get out of the minors.

the players picked ahead of Frank have become big stars.

Frank accepted a contract from the White Sox and left Auburn as the school's all-time leader in home runs, with 49. "He was the best player we ever had," says Coach Baird. "We loved him. He was fun to be around . . . always smiling, always bright-eyed. I never saw what I thought was a football player's mentality with Frank. He was very focused, but never in a head-banging way."

Frank began banging baseballs as a pro for the first time in the summer of 1989. He played 16 games for the White Sox's rookie league team, in Sarasota, Florida, where he batted .333, with 11 RBIs. He got a quick promotion to Sarasota's Class A team, in the Florida State League, the next level up. There he hit .277, with 4 homers and 30 RBIs in only 55 games.

Frank had made up his mind that he wasn't going to spend a lot of time in the minor leagues. He wanted to get to the majors as quickly as possible. It seemed as if he

HEAD TO HEAD

In 1986, Frank caught three passes for 45 yards as a tight end for the Auburn Tigers. He gave up football the next season because of ankle and knee injuries. Junior gave up football in high school because he didn't like being tackled!

"I was very crushed because the year before, I was the second-leading hitter on the team," Frank says. "I was like, 'What are you talking about, trying out?'"

Frank was so insulted, he stayed home that summer. Many of the players who competed in the 1988 Olympics, such as first baseman Tino Martinez and third baseman Robin Ventura, are now big leaguers. Robin is now Frank's teammate on the White Sox.

Not being invited to play in the Olympics, Frank says, "made me go back to outworking everyone else." He bounced back and had an incredible season for Auburn in 1989. He led the SEC in batting with a .403 average, and in RBIs with 83, and was named conference MVP.

Frank was such an amazing hitter that opposing players would stop their pregame exercises to watch him take batting practice. Some of his hits became so legendary that players often pointed to far-off spots where Frank's home runs had landed. Some blasts had even gone over the 45-foot-high scoreboard at Plainsman Park, Auburn's home field.

Major league scouts were once again watching Frank with great interest. This time they were not going to let him get away. On June 5, 1989, the Chicago White Sox made Frank the seventh player chosen in the major league draft. Even then, the scouts and the teams seemed to have underestimated Frank. Pitcher Ben McDonald, who is now with the Milwaukee Brewers, was chosen first, but none of season. He still thinks he would have made the NFL if he had kept playing, but the decision was a wise one. Pat Dye, Auburn's head football coach, let Frank keep his scholarship so he could stay in school and concentrate on baseball.

Frank made the most of his opportunity. During his sophomore season, in 1988, he won the Southeastern Conference batting championship with a .385 average. It was a great accomplishment because pitchers had become wise to how good Frank was and rarely gave him good pitches to hit. Sometimes Frank got frustrated.

"Frank finally started swinging at pitches three or four inches off the plate," says Hal Baird, Frank's baseball coach at Auburn.

Swinging at bad pitches made Frank strike out more. He had to remind himself to be patient. "My freshman and sophomore years, I wanted to hit home runs," he says. "Steve Renfro, my batting coach at Auburn, told me, 'Guys aren't going to serve pitches up on a platter for you. You've got to make them come in with something good.' I understood that I had to become more selective."

Frank was like a powerful locomotive gaining speed, but he ran into another disappointment during the summer of 1988. The U.S. National Baseball Team was preparing for the Summer Olympics, which would begin in Seoul, South Korea in September. Frank was sure he would be invited to join the team, but he was told he would have to try out.

three passes for 45 yards that season, but he gained a lot of valuable experience. Traveling around the country and playing in front of 90,000 fans prepared him for his future life in the major leagues. "It was an experience I wouldn't change for anything," Frank says.

In the spring of 1987, Frank tried out for Auburn's baseball team and made the roster at what was a new position for him: first base. He had an outstanding season, batting .359 and setting a single-season school record with 21 home runs.

That summer, Frank was invited to play for the U.S. National Baseball Team as it prepared for the 1987 Pan Am Games. Frank batted .474 in seven exhibition games, but returned to Auburn before the Pan Am Games started, in August, because he had to prepare for his sophomore season of football.

Playing football took a physical toll on Frank. He developed "spurs" (sharp, painful edges) in the bones of his ankles and needed surgery to remove them. Then, in a practice before his sophomore season, he was hit from behind by one of his teammates and hurt his right knee.

Frank began having second thoughts about playing football. "I watched some of my friends who were just so much more talented than me have their football careers end because of injury," he says. "Baseball gave me a chance at a long career, and I think I had more talent at baseball."

So Frank gave up football before his sophomore

STEPPING ON THE GAS

After graduating from high school in June 1986, Frank moved on to Auburn University, in Auburn, Alabama. He hadn't given up on a baseball career, but football now came first. He put all his effort into making the Auburn Tigers as a tight end, which might then lead to playing in the National Football League after college.

"I really made sure that I stood out in practice every day," Frank says, "making catches and making things happen."

In the classroom, Frank majored in business, but he also got an education on the football field. "Playing football for Auburn was a whole new world for me," he later told a reporter from *Sport* magazine. "It made me a man. I learned what hard work means."

That's a pretty amazing thought: Frank had already been a very hard worker!

Frank was honored when he made the football team. Usually, freshmen at Auburn were given a non-playing status on the team until the following year. Frank caught only would go to college instead and they would miss a chance to pick a player who only wanted to play baseball.

The scouts didn't know that Frank really wanted to play baseball. He quit playing basketball his senior year to work harder at baseball. Going to college was just a safety net he thought he should have in case he wasn't drafted. "I always tell kids to go to college," he says. "If you're not a first-round draft pick out of high school, go to college. It's something to fall back on."

On June 2, 1986, major league teams held their draft of amateur players. The draft lasted three days. A total of 1,423 players were chosen. Frank wasn't one of them. He was so upset, he went to his room and cried. "It was devastating," he says. "A number of guys who weren't even close to me in talent, they got drafted. The scouts goofed."

Yet, it didn't take Frank long to get over that big hurt. He just did what he always does when he wants to prove people wrong: He worked even harder.

guard and center. The following year, he made varsity and led the team in scoring. He also became a standout tight end and placekicker on the varsity football team.

Frank grew seven inches during the summer between his freshman and sophomore years. When he returned to school, he was a 6' 3" power-hitting monster who made the varsity baseball team easily. He hit .425 that season and led the Columbus High Blue Devils to their first-ever state championship. During his junior season, in 1985, Frank hit .329, with 8 homers and 23 RBIs. He was also named the city's high school player of the year.

Major league scouts were very impressed by Frank. His power was awe-inspiring. He hit home runs over the light poles at Columbus's home field! His coaches gave him nicknames like "Big Bopper" and "Hammer."

Along with being powerful, Frank was also smart. "He was a disciplined hitter from the start," says Bobby Howard, Frank's baseball coach at Columbus High. "Frank would never swing at a garbage pitch, even when the count was no balls and two strikes."

There was no question that Frank had the talent to become a pro baseball player, but the scouts were worried about recommending him as a draft choice. The scouts were concerned because Frank had signed a letter of intent to accept a scholarship to play football at Auburn University, in Alabama. They were afraid that if they drafted him, he

Since joining the White Sox, Frank has done a lot to help find a cure for leukemia. His charity foundation raises thousands of dollars each year. One of his best-known projects is "The Frankie Fund." Frank charges fans one dollar each time he signs an autograph and then matches the dollar with one of his own. Both dollars are donated to the Leukemia Society of America. As you can imagine, a popular player like Frank signs a lot of autographs each year.

After Pamela's death, Frank started working out and lost the pudgy stomach he had had. As his stomach flattened, his confidence grew. One day, Mr. Thomas was urging Frank's brother, Mike, to work out more and practice harder in football. "Daddy," Frank said, "Don't fuss with Mike. Mike's going to be the hardworking man. I'm going to be the athlete."

When Frank entered Columbus High School as a 15-year-old freshman, he was in great shape and very determined to make the varsity baseball team. He tried out and did well, but got a rude surprise: He was cut.

Frank later learned that he had no chance of making the team, no matter how good he was. The coaches did not allow freshmen on the varsity team, but they didn't tell Frank. "They just wanted to see what kind of talent they had coming along," he says. "It was tough. As I look back on it, it made me work harder to get better."

Frank played Babe Ruth baseball instead. On the freshman basketball team at Columbus High, he starred as a

18 FRANK THOMAS

Frank was heartbroken. "I was sad for a long time," he says. "She was my favorite person, but I learned to move on. Life moves on."

Pamela's death made Frank dedicate himself to sports. He wanted to honor her memory by becoming a great player. He also decided that if he ever became a major leaguer, he would use his fame and money to help battle leukemia.

"I remember him saying to me not long after Pamela died, 'Dad, maybe one day I'll be able to do something about it,'" Mr. Thomas told a reporter from *Sports Illustrated*.

HEAD TO HEAD

In 1978, the year Frank turned 10:
- The New York Yankees defeated the Los Angeles Dodgers in the World Series, 4 games to 2.
- Yankee slugger Reggie Jackson had a candy bar (the "Reggie!") named after him.
- "Space Invaders" was the hot new video game.
- Egypt and Israel signed a peace treaty at Camp David, Maryland.
- Junior was 9 years old and his dad was an outfielder for the Cincinnati Reds. Ken senior batted .288, with 10 homers, 63 RBIs, and 23 stolen bases that season.

because he could cover the whole outfield. Most kids didn't want to play the outfield, but with Frank, that became our glory position. He used to throw people out at first base from centerfield. If it was a hard line drive to center, the batter was as good as dead."

One day, after Frank had played well in football, his coach told Mr. Thomas, "This kid will be a pro athlete. I don't know in which sport, but he will be a pro athlete."

The sport turned out to be baseball, of course, but it wasn't until after Frank, still a boy, and his family suffered a terrible tragedy that he decided he wanted a career in pro sports.

On Labor Day, September 5, 1977, Frank's 2-year-old sister, Pamela, suddenly became so sick she couldn't walk. Doctors discovered she had leukemia, a serious blood disease that is often fatal.

Pamela was taken to Egleston Children's Hospital, in Atlanta, Georgia, where she was treated with powerful drugs that, as a side effect, made her hair fall out. Frank was very worried. He and Pamela were close, even though he was 9 and she was 2. They were, after all, the "babies" in the family. Frank called his mom at the hospital and asked, "When is Pamela coming home?"

Pamela came home a week or so later, and she gave Frank a big, beaming smile. But sadly, she never got better. She died on Thanksgiving Day that year.

they're better than you, because they aren't." Frank took those words to heart.

Frank was a big kid. By age 9, he was 5' 6" tall. He usually played against older kids. The competition was tough, and it forced him to improve. "I had to be able to play well so they'd let me play," he says. "Playing with an older crowd, that's the only way you're going to get better."

Frank was good. He was good enough at 9 to play against 12-year-olds in Pop Warner football. In Little League, pitchers were scared of him. "Kids would throw the ball behind him, over the backstop, all over the place," Mr. Thomas says. "They'd do anything to avoid pitching to him."

Jack Key, who coached Frank on the Peach Little League Lions, remembers how hard Frank used to hit the ball as a 12-year-old. "He hit rockets,'" Coach Key once said to reporter Guerry Clegg of *The Columbus Ledger-Enquire* newspaper. "He hit the longest ball I ever saw hit there. It went into the top of a pine tree. This was a shot that would have reached a major league warning track. And this was a Little League kid!"

Frank's throwing arm was as powerful as his bat. He played centerfield and also pitched for the Lions. He threw a no-hitter one day, but lost the game when he walked a batter and the catcher missed two pitches that allowed the runner to reach third and then score on a sacrifice fly.

"Frank could have played any position he wanted to," Coach Key said. "But we put him in centerfield money.) Mr. Thomas was also a deacon at a local Baptist church. His mom worked at a textile factory.

Frank's parents had to work during the day, so his brothers and sisters often took care of him. A typical day when he was a kid started with going to school, then playing sports until it got dark, then going home to eat dinner and do homework.

Frank spent most of his time playing at the local Boys Club. "I had to walk three or four miles down the railroad track to get there every day," he says. "I would go with my brother, Mike, and my friends would go, too."

Frank played a bunch of different sports. The Boys Club had baseball, football, and basketball teams that competed against three other local clubs. Frank's favorite sports were basketball and football, but he liked baseball, too. He rooted for the Atlanta Braves. One of his heroes was Hall of Fame slugger Hank Aaron, who holds the all-time major league career record of 755 home runs.

"I'm not bragging," Frank's dad once told *Sports Illustrated*, "but Frank did so well in all sports. And he loved them all. I never crammed them down his throat. I never had to worry about him. It didn't matter what time of day or night it was, I knew Frank was at the Boys Club or the playground, somewhere with a ball in his hands."

While Mr. Thomas didn't cram sports down Frank's throat, he did give his son a good deal of encouragement. Mr. Thomas often said, "Don't let anyone ever tell you

2
BIG BOPPER AND LITTLE PAMELA

Frank Edward Thomas, Junior, was born on May 27, 1968, in Columbus, Georgia. He was the fifth of Frank and Charlie Mae Thomas's six children. Frank has an older brother, Mike, and three older sisters — Gloria, Mary, and Sharon. A fourth sister, Pamela, was born seven years after Frank.

Frank grew up in Columbus, a medium-sized city of about 178,000 people located near the western border of Georgia. His family lived in a small house on Dunhill Drive. They didn't have a lot of money, but they always had things they needed. Frank's dad worked as a bail bondsman at a local jail. (People who have been arrested can pay bail money to stay out of jail until their trial. They can pay a bail bondsman a small percentage of their bail, and the bondsman puts up the rest. When the person goes to trial, the bondsman gets the bail money back, and keeps the percentage. If the person runs away, the bondsman loses the majors. "Frank is a great ballplayer," says five-time All-Star Ken Griffey, Junior. "Anytime you put up numbers like he has, you have to take your hat off. Every time he hits a home run, I laugh."

Junior has laughed a lot since Frank joined the White Sox in August 1990. And fans have spent a lot of time arguing about which one of these two sensational sluggers is better. Frank admires Junior, but he believes in himself most of all.

"You want to know how good I am?" Frank told sportswriter Murray Chass of *The New York Times,* in 1993. "Come out to the ballpark ten straight days and see how good I am. If that doesn't impress you, you have your own opinions. I've done damage to every pitcher in the league."

That sounds like boasting, but other people agree with Frank. White Sox TV broadcaster and former major leaguer Ken Harrelson says, "Thirty years from now, if you take a poll of a hundred hitters, they'll say 'Frank Thomas is the best hitter who ever lived.'"

school baseball team the first time he tried out. Then, after starring for Columbus High for three years, major league teams did not draft him. He went to Auburn University on a football scholarship instead, but later became the school's best baseball player. Later on, after he had been drafted and was playing in the minors, when he thought he was ready to make the White Sox in spring training in 1990, he was sent back to the minors.

That so many people doubted his ability seems crazy now because Frank is such an amazing hitter. But becoming a great hitter took a lot of work. Every time Frank failed to achieve one of his goals, he worked even harder to succeed the next time.

"I pride myself in proving people wrong," Frank says. "I hate when people tell me I can't do something. It makes me work a little harder. I'm not afraid to work."

Frank is an extremely confident person on and off the field. He runs his own business, Big Hurt Enterprises, and wants to be a successful businessman when he retires.

Frank is also a husband and father. He and his wife, Elise, live in Burr Ridge, Illinois, with their two kids, Sterling Edward (age 4) and Sloan Alexandra (2). Elise doesn't think of Frank as a superstar, but she admits her husband can be pretty awesome. "What amazes me is that he's so good day in and day out," Elise says.

Day in and day out, Frank is one of the best in the

"The hardest thing to teach is patience at the plate," White Sox batting coach Walt Hriniak *[RIN-ee-ack]* told reporter Robert Markus of *The Chicago Tribune* newspaper. "Frank is a little like [five-time American League batting champion] Wade Boggs. He wants to see as many pitches as possible. That's his style."

Frank may seem easygoing because he's willing to accept so many walks, but he is incredibly determined to succeed every time he is up. Even when he is hitting well, he gets upset with himself.

In a game against the Baltimore Orioles in 1991, Frank swung at a pitch that was high and outside and belted the ball 430 feet into the leftfield stands. After he trotted around the bases and returned to the dugout, Frank's teammates were surprised to see that he was upset. "I swung at ball four," he complained.

"Some of my teammates have told me, 'Frank, you're crazy,'" Frank says. "'You're hitting .300, so what are you worrying about?' I'm not crazy. I'm a competitor. I'm one of those guys who has to pour it on every night. If I get three hits, I'm disappointed that I didn't get four."

"I have never seen him give up an at-bat," says Coach Hriniak. "No matter if we're ten runs ahead or he's already gotten his four hits or two homers. He has an intense hatred of failure."

That hatred was born out of the disappointments Frank experienced in his life. He failed to make his high

There are many great major league power hitters such as Ken Griffey, Junior, of the Seattle Mariners, Matt Williams of the San Francisco Giants, Albert Belle of the Cleveland Indians, and Mo Vaughn of the Boston Red Sox. None are as patient at the plate as Frank.

The way Frank sees it, a walk is as good as a hit, and there's no use swinging at bad pitches. "If they want to send me down there [to first base], I'll go," he says. "I just learned to be patient. If a pitch isn't in the strike zone, I'm so picky I won't swing the bat."

That attitude has made Frank the smartest power hitter to come along since Hall of Famer Ted Williams *(see box below)*.

HEAD TO HEAD

Both Frank and Junior have been compared to Hall of Fame slugger Ted Williams. Ted, who was nicknamed "The Kid," as Junior is, played for the Boston Red Sox between 1939 and 1960. He batted .344, hit 521 homers, and drove in 1,839 runs. Like Frank, he had great patience at the plate and refused to swing at bad pitches. Ted received more than 100 walks in 11 different seasons. Frank has walked more than 100 times in each of his five full seasons.

eyes are one of the big reasons for his success. He concentrates on watching the ball come out of the pitcher's hand and can see it so clearly that sometimes the ball looks as if it were moving in slow motion. And Frank refuses to swing at pitches that are out of the strike zone, even if it means being walked instead of getting the chance to hit a home run.

"I don't go crazy over home runs," Frank has said. "I want good technique home runs. I concentrate on average and RBI. Those are what're important to me."

HEAD TO HEAD

Frank is one of only 11 players in major league history who have won back-to-back Most Valuable Player awards. The other 10 are:

Barry Bonds	Pirates, 1992; Giants, 1993
Dale Murphy	Braves, 1982, 1983
Mike Schmidt	Phillies, 1980, 1981
Joe Morgan	Reds, 1975, 1976
Roger Maris	Yankees, 1960, 1961
Ernie Banks	Cubs, 1958, 1959
Mickey Mantle	Yankees, 1956, 1957
Yogi Berra	Yankees, 1954, 1955
Hal Newhouser	Tigers, 1944, 1945
Jimmie Foxx	A's, 1932, 1933

mask and shin guards. Pitchers shouldn't be left out there alone with him."

Pitchers will do just about anything to avoid throwing to Frank. From 1991 through 1995, he averaged slightly over 125 walks per season. But Frank is much more than just a walking man. When he hits the ball, he kills it. That's one of the reasons his nickname is "The Big Hurt."

Frank has described himself as "a little picky, pesky hitter." Little? The Big Hurt is 6' 5" tall and weighs 250 pounds! His former White Sox teammate Steve Lyons once joked that "Frank is too big to be a man and too small to be a horse."

One thing is for sure: Frank has plenty of horsepower in his bat. During his first five full seasons with the White Sox, Frank batted .323, hit 35 home runs, and drove in 113 runs per season. He has played in three All-Star Games and was named the American League's Most Valuable Player in 1993 and 1994.

Frank is an awesome hitter to watch. When he steps to the plate, fans in every ballpark pay attention. Any swing of Frank's bat could produce a monster home run or a screaming hit. Of course, opposing teams don't enjoy watching or playing against The Big Hurt. When Milwaukee Brewer pitching coach Don Rowe was asked to name his favorite Frank Thomas at-bat, Don couldn't do it. "I usually cover my eyes," he said.

When it comes to hitting, Frank's eyes have it. Great

Dave definitely did not want to throw a pitch Frank could hit. If he did, the Blue Jays would likely end up watching the ball fly over the fence and find themselves behind, 4–2. So what was Dave going to do? How about walking Frank intentionally?

"Walk Frank Thomas?" Blue Jays catcher Pat Borders had said earlier that season, answering a question from a reporter. "I got no problem with that."

And that's exactly what Toronto did. Dave walked Frank, who trotted down to first as Chicago's first run of the game was forced home to score. Robin Ventura, the next batter, grounded out and another run scored. The game was tied, 2–2. But when Ellis Burks made the third out, Toronto escaped the jam and went on to win, 6–3.

"Walking me there, I thought it was pretty smart," Frank said after the game. "I wasn't going to let those men stay on base. Instead of getting two runs that inning, we should have had three or four."

Frank Thomas is such a tremendous hitter that walking him is just about the only way to keep him from winning games all by himself. A reporter from *Sports Illustrated* once asked Cleveland Indian manager Mike Hargrove how to pitch to Frank. "Throw it ten feet in front of the plate and hope he doesn't hit it on the first hop," Mike replied.

Indian pitcher Dennis Martinez says that facing Frank is so scary, "I wish they'd let us put on the catcher's

1

WALKING THE WALK

The bases were loaded with one out in the third inning and the 45,527 fans in Chicago's Comiskey Park were screaming. Slugging first baseman Frank Thomas was stepping up to the plate.

The Chicago White Sox were behind, 2–0, and down to the Toronto Blue Jays three games to two in the 1993 American League Championship Series. One more loss and the Sox would be eliminated. But their fans were confident. If there was one man they wanted at the plate, it was Frank.

Frank was the one man the Blue Jays *did not* want to see. He had batted .317, with 41 homers and 128 RBIs that season. Toronto pitchers had walked him eight times in his first 16 at-bats in the playoffs before he got a good pitch to hit in the sixth inning of Game 4. Frank crushed it for a home run that traveled 433 feet.

On the mound for Toronto was Dave Stewart, who had pitched in the majors for 14 seasons. Dave knew how to pitch in tense situations to good hitters. He had won 20 or more games in a season four times.

CONTENTS

1. Walking the Walk 6
2. Big Bopper and Little Pamela 14
3. Stepping on the Gas 22
4. The Big Hurt 30
5. MVP, Hands Down. 38
6. The Great Home Run Derby 47
7. Loving the Big Moments 57

   Frank Thomas's Career Stats 64

HEAD TO HEAD BASEBALL

FRANK THOMAS

by John Rolfe

A Sports Illustrated For Kids Book

TIMEOUT!

HEADS UP, BASEBALL FANS

HEAD-TO-HEAD BASEBALL is a unique kind of book; it has two fronts and no back. Choose the superstar you want to read about first, read his story, then flip the book over and read about the other player.

In the stories, you'll read how two very different players from two very different backgrounds ended up in the major leagues. You'll get the lowdown on the Chicago White Sox's sensational slugger, Frank Thomas, and the inside scoop on the Seattle Mariners' main man, Ken Griffey, Junior. After reading both athletes' stories, tackle the amazing center section of the book. This section has fantastic photos, complete statistics, and a comic strip, all of which show just how these two power hitters stack up against each other.

Okay, it's time for the first pitch. So pick The Big Hurt or Junior and get ready for all the Head-to-Head action!